How to
DRINK
LIKE A
RockStar

How to DRINK LIKE A ROCKSTAR

ALBERT W. A. SCHMID

RED ⚡ LIGHTNING BOOKS

This book is a publication of

Red Lightning Books
1320 East 10th Street
Bloomington, Indiana 47405 USA

redlightningbooks.com

Manufactured in the United States of America

ISBN 978-1-68435-107-7 (hdbk)
ISBN 978-1-68435-108-4 (web PDF)

1 2 3 4 5   25 24 23 22 21 20

THIS BOOK IS DEDICATED TO
my godmother,

BARBARA B. MILLER;

always a rock star!

CONTENTS

FOREWORD

WHEN ASKED ABOUT DRINKING LIKE a rock star, I am sure many think of extreme excess—you know, party till you puke. This mind-set did not work out very well for John Bonham, Bon Scott, or Amy Winehouse. Their deaths were from excess alcohol. Growing up, I was an avid reader of *Creem* and *Hit Parader* and do not recall ever seeing a photo of Jimmy Page without a bottle of Jack Daniel's somewhere in the shot. Excess!

During the summer of 1981, I saw Def Leppard open for Ozzy Osbourne's Blizzard of Ozz tour. I was not familiar with Def Leppard, but what sticks in my memory is the crew having to walk guitarist Pete Willis, who was obviously drunk, to the stage to help keep his balance. In 1982, Willis was fired due to excessive alcohol consumption "on the job." Steve Clark, Def Leppard's other guitarist, would battle alcoholism until his death in 1991. As for Ozzy, during the show, he was pretty much frozen center stage clutching his microphone stand with both hands. Wonder why? Excess!

Van Halen's bassist Michael Anthony even had a bass shaped like a Jack Daniel's bottle he played during the show. When I first moved to Los Angeles, I lived in Sherman Oaks at Ventura Boulevard and Woodman Avenue. Ventura Boulevard has countless liquor stores, and every one of them had an autographed photo from Edward Van Halen. Excess!

I, like many may, recall director Penelope Spheeris's *The Decline of Western Civilization Part II: The Metal Years*. In one of the key scenes, Spheeris interviews WASP's Chris Holmes while he floats in a pool sipping vodka and slurring; his mother sits poolside during the interview. Spheeris asks how much he drinks a day. Holmes replies, "About five pints." Excess!

While living in Los Angeles, I got my first big opportunity to work on a big-time record. Joe Zawinul, who worked with Weather Report and Miles Davis among others, asked me if I was available to engineer his new record. This was a no-brainer! We finished overdubs and mixed at his home studio in Malibu. Joe's wife, Maxine, prepared wonderful meals for us each day. We would break from recording and sit down at the dinner table for a proper meal. At the end of each meal, Joe would break out the after-dinner drink of choice: slivovitz! Drinking slivovitz (which is produced in Central and Eastern Europe) after a meal was a tradition in the Zawinul family. . We would slowly sip the slivo and savor it. This was classy!

From the fall of 1994 until the summer of 1997, I had a working relationship with the alternative rock band Porno for Pyros. My role began as engineer but morphed into producer, musician, and ultimately band member. We spent thirteen months working on the second album, *Good God's Urge*, at the Shangri-La Ranch in Zuma Beach. We had a chef who would prepare lunch and dinner for us. A poolroom had a fully stocked bar. A portion of this bar is seen on the album cover of Eric Clapton's *No Reason to Cry*. Note: When Clapton returned to music after the *Layla* sessions, he had given up drugs and took to excessive drinking. He was often very drunk at gigs and booed off the stage.

We (the band) spent little time in the poolroom/bar as we were working. However, we would often have drinks at our prepared lunch and dinner as part of the dining process.

Around Thanksgiving 1994, Perry Farrell and I went to the liquor store and bought some very fine bottles of scotch, including a forty-year-old Ballantine. During that holiday season, we enjoyed sipping the scotch at the end of the day's work. This continued through the holiday season and began again the next year. It became tradition and was never in excess.

Beginning late 1995, we began to tour. Our tour rider included various adult beverages, including Heineken, Stoli, Jim Beam, and Bacardi. As the tour progressed, we developed a huge stockpile of beverages. By October 1996, we had no more room to carry additional bottles. However, we did not have as much Jim Beam as the others. Bassist Mike Watt's philosophy was that bourbon was a "political drink." Watt is known for his work with the Minutemen and Iggy and the Stooges. If you were discussing politics and drinking, it had to be bourbon. While on the bus for hours and hours we had many discussions on politics, however, never in excess.

During the 1996 tour, we were in Seattle for a show at the Moore Theatre. After sound check, I was the last to exit the venue and witnessed Eddie Vedder quietly leave a bottle on Perry's vocal effect rack. This was a secret gift to Perry, and as usual, close to the end of the show, Perry shared with everyone.

My experience of drinking like a rock star was never in excess, but a process of being family, sharing with others, and tradition. Rock on!

> *Thomas "TJ" Johnson, Department Chair,*
> *Creative and Performing Arts, Guilford*
> *Technical Community College, former*
> *band member and producer for*
> *Porno for Pyros, and long-time*
> *industry veteran*

ACKNOWLEDGMENTS

I WISH TO THANK THE following:

My wife, Kim, for her love, support, and copyediting.

My sons, Tom and Mike, for always inspiring me to do my best.

My mother, Elizabeth Schmid, for all of her support and advice.

My sisters and brothers, Gretchen, Rachel, Justin, Bennett, Ana, Shane, and John, for their support.

My rock star colleagues, instructors, and professors in the Culinary Arts and Hospitality Management Departments at Guilford Technical Community College, including Linda Beitz, Michele Prairie, Al Romano, LJ Rush, Tom Lantz, and Keith Gardner. Samphanh Soxayachanh, rock star department administrative assistant; I enjoy starting my business day with your smile and happy nature.

My friend and former student, Loreal "the Butcher Babe" Gavin, whose enthusiasm is infectious.

My friend and attorney, Scot Duval, for his friendly counsel.

My friend Gary Gruver, mentor mixologist.

My friends Brian and Angie Clute—looking forward to the next trip!

My longtime friend Keith Mellage.

My friend Deb Walsh, Esq., for her energy, enthusiasm, and smile.

My friend and mentor, Lou Mongello; thank you for your advice and support and for giving Momentum to my projects and to me.

My Momentum accountability partners Erin King, David Tarnoff, and Scott Cornelius for their advice, support, and friendship.

The artists who made me laugh, smile, and dance while working on this project: Justin Timberlake, Jimmy Fallon, James Corden, Ellen DeGeneres, Bill Murray, Bill Burr, George Carlin, Etta James, Frank Sinatra, Alicia Keys, Jill Scott, Jay-Z, Dr. Dre, Bruno Mars, Maroon 5, Herb Alpert, Miles Davis, Michael Bublé, Snoop Dogg, Mark Ronson, Stacy Kent, Greta Van Fleet, and the others listed in this book!

ROCK STAR LEXICON

BENNETT "DJ BENNETT" SCHMID

THE FOLLOWING ARE TERMS RELATED to the world of rock 'n' roll.

A&R Short for artists and repertoire; a record label employee in charge of scouting and developing talent.

Analog A term used to describe how sound is recorded, amplified, or reproduced. Analog sound amplifies vibrations using tubes rather than modern electronics or a digital signal. Analog recording was often done in a single continuous take or made using multitrack recording and splicing takes together.

Arena rock A term used to encapsulate a number of different styles of rock bands from the 1980s and early 1990s that were known for big stage productions, light shows, and pyrotechnics and whose music is characterized by catchy sing-along pop hooks. Sometimes used derisively; examples include U2, Journey, Guns N' Roses, Van Halen, and AC/DC.

Axe Slang for a guitar.

Backbeat A steady rhythm that emphasizes the second and fourth beats in a four-note measure. A strong backbeat is one of the characteristics that defined rock music and was popularized by drummer and New Orleans native Earl Palmer, who recorded some of the most iconic records in the history of rock music for artists such as Fats Domino, Ray Charles, Sam Cooke,

Richie Valens, the Beach Boys, Ike and Tina Turner, and Neil Young.

Blues rock A style of rock music rooted in the guitar sounds of the Mississippi Delta and Chicago blues traditions. American blues music was one of the primary influences for bands ranging from Led Zeppelin to Fleetwood Mac to Black Sabbath to Pink Floyd and to Jimi Hendrix. Austin-based artist Gary Clark Jr. is considered by many to be the standard bearer for modern blues rock today.

Bridge The metal bracket on the lower body of a guitar, which elevates the strings to a certain set height above the pickup and fret board. Also, in rock and pop music, the bridge of a song refers to a part of the song that does not repeat itself, which often follows the second verse or chorus and is sometimes marked or followed by a key change.

British Invasion A group of British rock and pop bands from the late 1960s, such as the Beatles, the Kinks, the Rolling Stones, the Who, and the Yardbirds, who helped popularize rock music as a dominant cultural phenomenon in popular American culture. The British Invasion bands were primarily influenced by American R&B, soul, blues, and rock 'n' roll.

CBGB A nightclub in New York City that was an integral part of the city's music scene, hosting concerts by some of the best-known punk, new wave, metal, and hardcore acts early in their careers, such as the Ramones, the Talking Heads, Blondie, the Misfits, Television, and Joan Jett and the Blackhearts.

China A large crash cymbal with a bright tone, somewhat reminiscent of a gong, which is commonly used for dramatic effect in rock or heavy metal music.

Chops Slang term used to describe a musician with a masterful skill for playing a wide variety of different rhythmic patterns or melodic riffs with precision. Example "That drummer had some mean chops!"

Cover song A performance of a song originally written by another artist. A cover song may be close to the original song arrangement or may be drastically different in tempo, sound, and style. Example 1980s synthpop group Soft Cell's cover of "Tainted Love" was originally written and recorded by Gloria Jones in 1964.

Crossroads A common blues rock trope based on Robert Johnson's song "Crossroad Blues." Johnson was said to have sold his soul to the devil for his talents, a story that has had enormous influence on generations of rock, blues rock, and heavy metal musicians.

Electric Ladyland The famed recording studio in New York City built for Jimi Hendrix, which has been home to iconic studio recordings in rock, R&B, disco, and hip hop from artists such as the Clash, D'Angelo, Blondie, Chic, David Bowie, John Lennon, and Stevie Wonder.

Encore A short set of usually less than a handful of songs that follows the main performance. After the band/ artist leaves the stage for a break following the main set, they will often return to play a few more of their best-known songs or occasionally a cover of a song from another artist.

EP Abbreviation for extended play vinyl, a term used to describe a short collection of a few songs typically not featured on a full-length album or CD release. An EP is often released between full-length albums and may feature alternate versions of a single, covers, B sides, or studio outtakes. Example Metallica's The $5.98

E.P. Garage Days Re-Revisited EP features a collection of five cover songs recorded following the death of bass player Cliff Burton between the group's albums Master of Puppets and . . .And Justice For All.

Fan Short for fanatic. A music lover with a deep fascination, admiration, or obsession with a particular artist or group. "I'm your biggest fan! I have every one of your albums. Even that rare limited-edition EP."

Fill A short rhythmic embellishment in time that adds to the backbeat or groove. A drum roll or cymbal accent that adds hits between notes to fill out the measure.

Funk rock A more upbeat, break-heavy style of rock music with a more prominent rhythm section than pop tock. Played by bands such as Sly and the Family Stone, the James Gang, the Clash, and Baby Huey & the Babysitters.

Ghostwriter A songwriter who writes songs for other performing artists. Example Max Martin has written the major hits for pop artists such as Justin Timberlake, the Weeknd, Taylor Swift, Katy Perry, and Adele, but is largely unknown as a performer.

Gig Slang among working musicians for a scheduled performance, often at a smaller venue in a casual setting rather than a large concert. Example Bob Dylan used to play two gigs a night at a small pub in Upper East Side Manhattan for a small fee plus a burger and two orders of french fries (source Bob Dylan exhibit at the Skirball Cultural Center).

Glam A style of rock music that became popular in the 1970s associated with colorful, flamboyant, or androgynous costumes and makeup. Some examples of 1970s glam rock artists are T. Rex, David Bowie, Alice Cooper, and Queen.

Grunge A raw style of rock music that arose in the punk and metal scene of the Pacific Northwest, partly as a rejection of the excesses of hair metal, with a grittier, distorted guitar sound and more aggressive rhythm. Defined largely by Seattle's Sub Pop label in the 1990s and made popular by bands such as Nirvana, Soundgarden, Melvins, Mudhoney, 7 Year Bitch, L7, and the Smashing Pumpkins.

Hair metal A style of popular rock music from the 1980s heavily influenced by 1970s glam rock aesthetics with a heavier guitar sound. Popularized in part by bands associated with Los Angeles's Sunset Strip music scene, such as Poison, Mötley Crüe, L.A. Guns, and Quiet Riot, who wrote songs about bikes, babes, heavy drinking, partying, and drugs.

Hardcore A subgenre of the punk scene that incorporates elements of heavy metal and thrash. Characterized by heavy, straightforward guitar riffs and quick-paced rhythms. Song themes are often antiauthoritarian, anti-fascist, or otherwise political in nature. Many hardcore bands embrace a lifestyle antithetical to the excess of mainstream rock music and abstain from hard alcohol and drug abuse. Examples Sick of It All, Minor Threat, Black Flag, Bad Brains, and the early incarnation of the Beastie Boys.

Heavy metal A style of rock music often known for using the shock value of occult imagery or subject matter and defined by distorted guitars and a heavy-handed style of drumming. Early heavy metal (or simply metal) acts include bands of the 1970s with a bluesy influence, such as Black Sabbath and Deep Purple.

Hook The chorus or refrain of a song that is easily remembered and draws the listener in. A good hook should stick with a listener after only one or two listens.

House of Blues An iconic music concert venue franchise that began in Massachusetts and has had iconic locations in numerous cities, most notably in Los Angeles on the Sunset Strip, in New Orleans within the French Quarter, in Chicago, and on the Las Vegas Strip. The House of Blues has hosted concerts for major rock and hip hop artists and has been mentioned in dozens of song lyrics. Example The Notorious B.I.G.'s "Going Back to Cali" mentions, "Sipping on booze in the House of Blues."

Indie rock A term originally used in the 1980s and 1990s to describe music released on independent record labels, such as SST, Dischord, Sub Pop, 4AD, or Matador Records, which gained popularity in part to heavy airplay on college radio stations. The term is now often used loosely to describe bands who are primarily influenced by underground aesthetics and music culture rather than popular commercial radio.

Jam An unrehearsed performance of new music. Also, an improvised arrangement of old music that differs from the original arrangement as it was rehearsed or recorded.

Kick A slang term that refers to the bass drum, which is played when the drummer steps on (or kicks) the bass drum pedal.

Knocks Slang used to describe a hard-hitting drumbeat or break. Example "That drum break at the beginning of 'When the Levee Breaks' knocks!"

LP Abbreviation for long player vinyl album. A full-length record release generally containing more than eight songs. However, some LPs may have far more or far fewer songs depending on the individual length of each song.

Power ballad A popular style of songwriting among rock bands of the 1970s and 1980s that opens with sparse or minimal arrangements, often using acoustic guitar or piano, and has a dramatic build accented by heavy guitars in the chorus. Examples Led Zeppelin's "Stairway to Heaven" and Journey's "Don't Stop Believin'."

Psychedelic rock Rock music that seeks to recreate the feeling of heavy intoxication from alcohol and psychoactive or hallucinogenic drugs. The term psych rock often refers to more obscure bands known for repetitive improvised jams often using experimental tones or otherwise unusual sounds, but major rock acts such as the Beatles, Pink Floyd, the Doors, Iron Butterfly, Jimi Hendrix, and even the Beach Boys all have some work that can be said to contain elements of psychedelic rock.

Punk A stripped-down form of rock music created with an aggressive style, often played by self-taught musicians. Punk rock is frequently associated with disaffected working-class youth movements.

Riff Slang term to describe the primary chord pattern that makes up the melody of a song. It generally refers to guitar, but can also be used to describe a horn melody, piano, or other instrument. Also, to play a variation on a common theme. Example "We were riffing on the twelve-bar blues."

Rockabilly A subgenre of rock 'n' roll with influences of country music, rhythm and blues, and swing. It is associated with early rock 'n' roll and country icons such as Elvis Presley, Johnny Cash, and Carl Perkins.

Session player A musician hired to perform on the studio recording of a song who is not a regular part of a performing act's live show or tour. Example Carol Kaye played bass guitar on dozens of popular pop, rock, soul, and television soundtrack sessions as a session player for Capitol Records' Wrecking Crew (see also Wrecking Crew).

Setlist The order in which an artist plays songs from their catalog at a live performance. Most performers or bands open with newer or lesser known material, saving their biggest hit songs and crowd pleasers for the end of the set or an encore.

Single A music release consisting of only one song, sometimes released with an instrumental or a B side. A single release is generally the record label's pick as the song with the greatest potential of chart success and is often released to create anticipation of an upcoming full-length album.

Solo A performance to spotlight an individual musician's skills (or chops). Example "Cliff Burton's bass solo on 'For Whom the Bell Tolls' absolutely shreds!"

Stack An amplifier containing four twelve-inch speaker cones (a half stack) or eight twelve-inch speaker cones (a full stack).

Surf rock A style of rock music, most often instrumental, that is known for guitar sounds that use echo and reverb effects to create a spacey vibe that is meant to evoke both the intensity and calm of being in the ocean. Surf rock guitarist Dick Dale is best known for his speedy style of intense guitar picking. The early work of the Beach Boys combines elements of surf rock and Southern California beach culture with doo-wop vocal harmonies. Surf rock has influenced the sounds of indie bands such as the Pixies and Khruangbin.

TBA To be announced, an acronym that appears on show flyers to note unconfirmed guests or opening acts.

27 Club The name given to a group of musical and cultural icons, including Jim Morrison, Janis Joplin, Amy Winehouse, Kurt Cobain, Robert Johnson, Jimi Hendrix, Jesse Belvin, and Jean Michel Basquiat, who all passed away at the age of twenty-seven. Most of the members of the 27 Club died at the height of their fame, most often due to the excesses of alcohol and drugs.

Whisky a Go Go Perhaps the most pivotal nightclub and concert venue in the development of the Los Angeles rock scene, the Whisky a Go Go on the Sunset Strip has hosted concerts for some of the most important rock music acts for more than fifty years. The Doors, Van Halen, X, Guns N' Roses, Mötley Crüe, Soundgarden, and dozens more acts are associated with the Whisky, as it is often called.

Wrecking Crew A small, famous group of session musicians who played on many of the most recognizable hits of the 1960s, 1970s, and 1980s.

How to
DRINK
LIKE A
RockStar

ONE

Drink Like a Rock Star

PRIMA FACIE, ROCK STARS LIVE by their own set of rules that sometimes looks like no rules at all. However, there are rules to being a rock star even if the rules are not immediately apparent. To decode these rules, perhaps the best place to begin is with the rock stars themselves. What do they think of their lifestyle? What rules do they live by? When Nickelback released the song "Rockstar" in 2005, they had an instant chart-busting hit on their hands. Many people could relate to the idea of aspiring to be one of the chosen few who become rock stars. The video seemed to bolster this success and featured a mix of rock stars and fans lip-syncing the words to the song in front of landmarks in large cities like New York, Chicago, Sydney, London, Berlin, and Los Angeles. Some of the rock stars featured in the video include Kid Rock, Gene Simmons, Ted Nugent, John Rich (who smashes a guitar), Twista, Nelly Furtado, and Billy Gibbons, to name a few. The song outlines the perceived benefits that rock stars enjoy: a large hilltop house with a huge bathroom, multiple high-end cars, a credit card with no spending cap, a private jet with a bedroom, being able to cut in line whenever you want to, free food, hanging out with movie stars in the VIP areas of clubs, and a star on Hollywood Boulevard. The song and the fun video tempt most to at least try the rock star lifestyle.

The rock star lifestyle appears easy to achieve and even easier to live. The 1985 single "Money for Nothing" explores the rock star lifestyle from the point of view of an outsider looking in. Two workingmen lament, "I shoulda learned to play the guitar. I shoulda learned to play them drums," because then they would have been millionaires with their own jet plane receiving "money for nothin' and the chicks for free." From the workingmen's point of view, the only perceived work hazards of rock stars are blisters on a thumb or little finger. Gordon Sumner (aka Sting) sings background and enjoys a songwriting credit with Dire Straits' lead singer Mark Knopfler. Marshall Mathers III (aka Eminem) takes the point of view of the performer in his 2003 Academy Award–winning original song, "Lose Yourself." With the idea of performing, "his palms are sweaty, knees weak, arms are heavy, there's vomit on his sweater already . . . but on the surface he look calm and ready." The crowd is screaming, and he knows that if he does not perform to his potential, he will be "booed off stage," so "success is his only motherfucking option." He knows that success lies on the other side of losing himself "in the music, the moment." Eminem also takes time to discuss how difficult a rock star's life is on the "lonely roads": going home, he has to reacquaint himself with his daughter. This gamble could pay off, but if he stops writing songs that become hits with the fans and on the charts, the fame, the fortune, and everything could end. He uses the idea and fear of failure as motivation for further success.

Joe Walsh sings about being a rock star in his song "Life's Been Good," which resonated with fans when it was released in 1978. The song opens to several drumbeats and an iconic guitar riff. The song is about a rock star who seemingly has everything, including gold records on his office wall. His large house goes unlived in because he is always on the road touring, living in hotels—but his friends tell him the house is "nice." Everyone says he is crazy because he is destroying the hotel rooms, but he says he is just having a good time trying to remember what happened (in part, because he is staying out late at parties drinking). He never seemingly takes responsibility because the accountants pay for everything. He never returns phone calls even though people leave messages for him. He owns a high-end car, but he can't drive it because he lost his license for excessive speeding. He is chauffeured in a limo that has locking doors so that he is not attacked by his fans, who think he is great. In the end, life's been good to him . . . so far.

Many other rock stars have written songs about the work-life balance of their chosen profession. In 1991, Tom Petty covered the rise and fall of a rock star with "Into the Great Wide Open"; the video features a young Johnny Depp. Bad Company asks how long will the celebrity last in their 1975 song "Shooting Star." Sheryl Crow and Kid Rock sang a duet in 2002, "Picture," about a rock star on the road and his girlfriend at home. Dr. Hook and the Medicine Show ruminate on Shel Silverstein's measure of a rock star's success by who could get on "The Cover of 'Rolling Stone.'" George Michael's 1990 hit "Freedom! '90" covers the choice of being a rock star: "Well it looks like the road to heaven but feels like the road to hell. When I knew which side my bread was buttered I took the knife as well. Posing for another picture, everyone's got to sell." Pink Floyd considers all the choices that rock stars have to make with their money in their 1979 song "What Shall We Do Now?" The Who contemplates how much money a band earns for themselves and how much they earn for the government (in the form of taxes) in their 1975 release "Success

Story." David Bowie discusses "Fame" in his 1975 hit by the same name. Bob Seger's 1973 hit "Turn the Page" envisages a rock star's life on the road. In 1998, Metallica would cover Segar's song. Counting Crows examine fame in "Mr. Jones," invoking the name of a rock legend, the person we all aspire to be, Bob Dylan. Rod Stewart supported Walsh's version of the rock star lifestyle when he mentioned to the host of the *The Late Late Show with James Corden* during a carpool karaoke that his group did destroy hotel rooms in part because the band did not get any respect from the hotels. In the movie *Begin Again*, which stars James Corden, Keira Knightley, and Adam Levine, about a group of emerging songwriters and rock stars, Levine's character, Dave Kohl, has a voice message stating that he is most likely doing something "awesome," so leave him a message and he "probably won't be able to get back to you . . . at all . . . ever," which also reinforces Walsh's warning of the hazards and pitfalls of the rock star life.

Any way you want to look at it—if you fantasize about changing your life for "fortune and fame" even though it may be tough to handle, growing your hair out or cutting it, changing your name or keeping it the same, or "livin' like a rockstar" like Post Malone and 21 Savage—you might want to follow some rules:

RULES FOR DRINKING COCKTAILS LIKE A ROCK STAR

Change your name . . . or don't—Some rockers choose to change their names, and others don't. For example, Joan Jett was born Joan Marie Larkin, but Glenn Frey chose to keep his given name. There are many examples of rock stars taking on new names, but there is an equal number of rock stars who have not. The way that you choose to go on this one is entirely up to you.

Live without regrets Everyone has a past, and we all mess up. This can be where great stories or life lessons originate. Life is still awesome; most of the time, no one notices or cares about little screw-ups. If they do notice, it usually only lasts one news cycle. As Gary Allen sings, in his song "No Regrets," "No regrets and peace of mind."

Practice makes playing better Always remember that the more you practice, the better you will play live. This is true for music and for mixing drinks. As soul singer Dionyza (Sutton) sings in her song "Practice Makes Perfect," "Practice makes perfect. Come on, let's get it right!"

Crank up the volume Life is short, and the average career of a rock star is much shorter: on average, about five years. So enjoy! You don't know how much longer this is going to last. "Crank it up! Put some of that party in my cup!" sings Colt Ford. Ashley Tisdale will also tell you, "Crank it up! Till the walls cave in!"

Walk to the beat of your own drum This is what separates a rock star from a rocker! You can't be a rock star if you copy someone else. Find your own style and your own rhythm, and enjoy life. "Hey, let's cheers to us. We're gonna be victorious. Don't matter what they say because we march to a beat of a different drum!" sings Sleeping with Sirens.

Do what you love, and love what you do Love it or leave it! If you don't love and find joy in what you are doing, perhaps it is time to change things up. One way to love what you do is make it your own and own it! Love is powerful. Huey Lewis declares that love is "tougher than diamonds and stronger than steel."

Be a free bird Lynyrd Skynyrd sang it all in their hit "Free Bird": free birds will "never change."

Own your fears Success is scary. To quote Taylor Swift, "Haters gonna hate," so "shake it off!" The only way to become a rock star is to own your fears. You got this one!

Set your goals Set your goals, then don't settle for less. If you want to tour the world, set the goal, then do it! As Freddie Mercury and Queen sing, "Don't stop me now!" And have a good time!

Surround yourself with a good band It matters who you take on your journey. You want reliable bandmates who will continually back you up and always sound good. As Yes sings, "Don't surround yourself with yourself," and "Just remember that the goal is for us all to capture all we want."

Do hard things that scare you Hard things scare everyone. If they didn't, everyone would be a rock star. Carrie Newcomer sings, "You can do this hard thing. It's not easy, I know, but I believe that it's so."

Live in the moment Jason Mraz sings, "I can't walk through life facing backwards," in his song "Living in the Moment." It's a great reminder that we need to let go of the past and enjoy what is happening right now.

You will fail Everyone does! Lit sings, "It's no surprise to me I am my own worst enemy." The key is to learn and turn the failure into a success.

Have fun "Let's burn up the night" like Kool and the Gang in the song "Big Fun." Life is too short not to have fun. With the right group of people, fun is easy!

Don't listen to the noise You are great! There is no question about that, but so are many other people; make sure you celebrate them too! Listen to AC/DC and say to someone, "Have a drink on me."

Don't believe your own hype Leonard Cohen wrote the song "Hallelujah" about great people who have foibles and how returning to one's center is very important. As great as we become, we need to remember at the end of the day we are just human. An amazing version of this song is performed by the Grammy Award–winning acapella group Pentatonix.

Always remember where you came from The duo Montgomery Gentry sings, "This is my town." No matter how famous you become, remember where you came from.

Finally, know your limits!

In addition to the fame and fortune, one of the best benefits of being a rock star is that you get to write your own rules! However, those rock stars who plan to create their own bars at home or who already have bars might consider checking or double-checking to make sure that they have the following items to maximize their and their guests' experiences.

MENU

Write a menu of the drinks that you feel confident you can make when your friends visit. Make sure these are drinks that you can produce quickly and with little effort so that you don't spend time flipping through books. For example, David A. Embury, the author of *The Fine Art of Mixing Drinks*, which was published in 1948, writes that the average host "can get along very nicely" knowing how to make six good cocktails. He suggests the gin martini, the Manhattan, the old-fashioned, the daiquiri, the sidecar, and the Jack Rose, all of which still work almost fourscore years later. Start small and simple with one drink. Once you have perfected the one, set a goal for five drinks; then expand to ten drinks as you learn them and set the goal of twenty drinks later. Spend time studying drinks away from the bar so that you can expand your menu. A menu will keep you focused and will keep your inventory small and focused too. The more drinks you add to that list, the more inventory that you need on hand so that you can produce the drinks on that menu.

SETTING THE BAR

Make sure you have the correct equipment for your bar. You might include one or more of each of the following pieces of equipment. Rock stars are confident and always have the correct gear for the gig. They come to the venue prepared.

Bar mat Bar mats come in assorted sizes and assorted colors, which means you can look for the perfect mat to match your bar or the decor of your home. Bar mats provide a stable, slip-free place to mix drinks. Also, they will contain spills and protect the surface below the mat.

Barspoon The barspoon is one of the most important tools of a bartender. Generally, the barspoon is a very long spoon, about eleven inches, with a twisted handle with a spoon at one end and a disk at the other. The twisted handle aids the bartender in stirring a drink in a mixing glass. The disk can be used to muddle soft items in the bottom of the glass and can be used to layer different alcohols in a glass for a classic layered drink.

Blender Every house and bar should have a blender, no matter what you think of blended drinks. There are some drinks that really should be blended. If you are going to use a blender, make sure to use ice that is already crushed to ensure you add years to the blades and the overall life of the blender. Examples of blended drinks include the margarita, the piña colada, and daiquiris.

Channel knife A channel knife is a small tool that helps the bartender create citrus twists. The blade of the tool cuts perfect twists both short and long to garnish drinks.

Citrus squeezer Fresh fruit juice makes a cocktail. The citrus squeezer is a tool that comes in numerous sizes specifically for limes, lemons, and other citrus fruits such as oranges and grapefruit. The tool acts as a lever that closes around the fruit, squeezing the juice out of the fruit.

Corkscrew A good corkscrew is important to have on hand to remove corks and bottle caps from bottles. The twisted "worm" is inserted into the cork to grab the cork for removal.

Ice Ice is a tool as well as part of the drink. Ice helps cool the drink quickly as well as chill the glass. Ice comes in diverse sizes and shapes. Bartenders should choose the ice size and shape based on the drink being created. Generally, ice comes in three shapes: cubed, crushed, and shaved. Today, there are many choices for molds and cut ice.

Ice scoop Ice should always be scooped into a glass. An ice scoop is a handled scoop that allows the bartender to effortlessly move ice from the ice bin to the mixing glass or to the drinking glass.

Jigger A jigger is a small two-sided hourglass-shaped measuring cup that is used to quickly and accurately measure out various portions of liquor, liqueur, juice, and other liquids to make cocktails. Most common jiggers are 1 ½ ounces on the large side and 1 ounce or less on the small side.

Julep strainer The julep strainer is a curved plate strainer made from stainless steel that is used to strain drinks from the mixing glass when there is no need for a fine strain.

Knife and cutting board A sharp paring knife should always be part of a properly equipped bar. Knifes are used to cut fruit and make garnishes. The cutting board should be small, just large enough to hold a piece of fruit.

Muddler A muddler is a small bat-shaped stick of wood or rod of metal. The muddler is used to crush sugar cubes and citrus fruits so they can be incorporated into the drink.

Napkins Napkins add a little class to the drink and will collect any condensation on the outside of the glass so that it does not damage the surface on which the glass is sitting. The color and design of the napkin can coordinate or contrast the bar.

Pour spout For a professional-looking bar, each bottle should be outfitted with a pour spout. This tool allows the bartender to create a consistent flow of liquid from any bottle. This reliable flow allows the bartender to reduce waste when pouring drinks.

Shaker Bartenders use two distinct types of shakers: the Boston shaker and the cobbler shaker. The Boston shaker comes in two parts: the tin and the mixing glass. If you use a Boston shaker, you will also need to purchase a strainer to hold the ice in the glass when straining the drink into the glass. The cobbler shaker is self-contained shaker, tin, and strainer all in one.

Small mesh strainer A small mesh strainer is used to strain out small chips of ice from a drink that is already being strained from a mixing glass or shaker. Sometimes this is referred to as the double strain.

Strainer A drink should always be served over fresh ice, which means a drink that is mixed or shaken should be strained from the mixing glass or the shaker into a glass that contains fresh ice. For a drink that is served straight up, the drink should be strained into a glass that has been chilled with a mixture of ice cubes and water.

Straws Bartenders use straws as tools in several ways. The straw can be a useable garnish for a drink. The straw gives the drink a finished look and provides the guest a way to sip the drink without touching his or her lips to the side of the glass. The other use for a straw is for sampling the drink. The bartender can dip the straw into the drink and then put a finger over the top of the straw to create a vacuum that will hold the liquid. The bartender can then taste the drink through the open end of the straw. Many bartenders use this technique to make sure that the balance of the drink is correct and that the drink tastes the way it should taste.

Swizzle sticks Swizzle sticks are used for built drinks, especially drinks from the Caribbean. The swizzle stick is used to mix a drink.

INGREDIENTS

Vodka Vodka is a non-aged, clear, distilled spirit with no aroma and no flavor. Vodka can be made from most anything with sugar. Bartenders like vodka because this neutral spirit sells well and mixes into drinks like a dream.

Gin Gin is a non-aged, clear, distilled spirit with a very distinct flavor and aroma. Gin starts off as a neutral spirit. Each gin is different, but most will have juniper berry in the flavor and aroma. Many mixed drinks are made with gin.

Rum Rum is a distilled spirit that can be non-aged or aged. Made from sugar cane, rum is an excellent mixer.

Tequila Tequila is a distilled spirit that can be non-aged or aged. This spirit is made from the agave plant. Unlike all the other spirits that are made from the annual crops of the world, tequila's agave takes almost a decade to grow. Great planning goes into tequila's production.

Brandy Brandy is a distilled spirit that can be non-aged or aged. Brandy is made from fruit wine, in most cases grape wine. Many popular brandies are aged in casks that give a golden color to the brandy.

Whiskey Whiskey is a distilled spirit that can be non-aged or aged. Whiskey is made from grain beer. All types of grains are used to make whiskey, although certain whiskeys require specific grains.

Liqueurs A liqueur is a sweetened, flavored spirit that is often used as a mixer, although liqueurs can be consumed by themselves before or after a meal. Flavors vary; fruits, nuts, and herbs make up most of the liqueurs on the market.

Fortified wine Fortified wine is wine with brandy added to raise the alcohol content. Originally for storage and shipping, the increased alcohol also makes a terrific addition to a cocktail.

Fresh juice Cocktails are better with fresh-squeezed juice. Most cocktails that feature juice contain a citrus juice: lime, lemon, orange, or grapefruit. Make sure you have enough to make cocktails for your party. Make sure that cocktails with juice are shaken.

Garnishes Most cocktails have prescriptive garnishes. For example, the Tom Collins always comes with an orange slice and a cocktail cherry, which is the same garnish for the old-fashioned. The Manhattan is garnished with a cocktail cherry, and the horse's neck comes with a long lemon twist. Make sure you know the proper garnishes and have plenty of garnishes for your party.

Some of the recipes you will make will call for simple syrup, which is simple and cheap to make. Some recipes call for sugar and water, but simple syrup will save time and will ensure that the sugar is completely dissolved. Here is a recipe for a good simple syrup to make at home.

Homemade Simple Syrup

1 cup water
1 ½ cups sugar

Place both the water and the sugar into a small pot. Bring the mixture to a boil for three minutes; then take the resulting syrup off the heat and let cool. Put the syrup into a plastic bottle and use as needed. Yield: about 2 cups.

Anytime a drink calls for lime juice or lemon juice and simple syrup, you can substitute sour mix. For example, if the drink calls for 1 ounce of lemon juice and ½ ounce simple syrup, then 1 ½ ounces of sour mix can be used instead. The following is a good sour mix to use at a home bar and builds on the knowledge of making simple syrup.

Homemade Sour Mix

1 ½ cups sugar
1 cup water
1 cup fresh-squeezed lemon juice
½ cup fresh-squeezed lime juice
½ cup fresh-squeezed orange juice

Squeeze enough lemons, limes, and oranges to have the needed quantity of juice. Mix the juice and refrigerate. Make the simple syrup with the sugar and the water by boiling for three minutes. Cool the simple syrup; then add to the fresh-squeezed juice.

Grenadine is a sweet and tart syrup used to flavor and color drinks a shade of red or pink. The origin of the word *grenadine* comes from the French word *grenade*, which means *pomegranate*. This is an easy recipe to make and will elevate drinks beyond the store-bought version.

*H*OMEMADE GRENADINE

1 cup pomegranate juice (no sugar added)
1 ½ cups sugar
½ teaspoon fresh lemon juice

Pour the sugar and the pomegranate juice into a pot. Warm, stirring the whole time, until the sugar dissolves into the juice. Pull from heat and allow to cool. Once cool, add the lemon juice. Store in bottles or jars under refrigeration. Use as needed. Yield: 2 cups.

There are some very good cocktail cherries on the market. If cherries are in season, you might try making them yourself. Here is an easy recipe that will get you started.

*H*omemade Cocktail Cherries

40 fresh cherries
¼ teaspoon cinnamon
2 cups plus ¼ cup bourbon (or your favorite spirit)

Pit the cherries. Heat a pan on the stove, pour the cherries into the pan, and sauté in the ¼ cup bourbon. If the cherries catch the flame, remove from the stove until the flame burns out. Add the cinnamon and mix. Pour the cherries into a sanitized jar and cover with bourbon. Allow to cool and refrigerate. Serve with your favorite cocktail that calls for a cocktail cherry.

*H*omemade Orgeat Syrup

1 cup almond milk
1 cup simple syrup
1 teaspoon orange flower water
1 ounce bourbon

Mix the almond milk and simple syrup together. Add the bourbon and orange flower water, stir together, and then let sit for twenty-four hours. Use as directed in cocktails.

GLASSWARE

Champagne flute A champagne flute is a tall drink glass designed to hold sparkling wine. With a narrow opening at the top, the glass effectively holds the CO_2 and releases the gas slowly, which allows for tiny streams of bubbles floating to the top of the glass. This glass is great for many cocktails, including the Seelbach cocktail and the French 75.

Cocktail glass Also known as a martini glass, this is the perfect vessel for a chilled drink served straight up. The V-shaped glass is iconic.

Highball glass Perfect for long drinks, this tall glass holds ice as well as at least ten ounces of liquid.

Hurricane glass An hourglass-shaped glass used for the hurricane cocktail and other drinks.

Margarita glass A glass specifically for the margarita, it has a large flat bowl at the top.

Mug This is a large vessel used for beer and cocktails.

Mule mug This distinctive copper mug is traditionally used for the mule family of drinks.

Old-fashioned A glass with straight sides and a flat bottom, it is also known as a low-ball glass or a rocks glass.

Pilsner glass The pilsner glass is perfect for a glass of beer or for a beer cocktail.

Pint glass The pint glass is used for beer and other cocktails.

Red wine glass This is a wine glass with a large bowl on top and a long stem.

Shot glass This small glass holds between 1 and 2 ounces or a shot of spirits.

White wine glass This is a wine glass with a small bowl on top and a long stem.

Bartenders use several techniques to make drinks properly. Each drink calls for a specific technique. Knowing how to complete drinks using these techniques will increase street credibility for the home bartender.

TECHNIQUES

Blending Using the blending technique is important for blended drinks such as the blended margarita, daiquiri, or piña colada. Blending is important for incorporating thick dairy products and whole or frozen fruit. Try to use less ice; too much ice will water down the finished drink. A happy medium is to use some ice and frozen fruit to maximize the flavor of the drink. Crushed ice should always be used for this technique to help extend the life and blades of the blender. When using crushed ice, be sure to blend for twenty seconds, stop, then blend for ten seconds.

Building Building a drink is simply pouring one ingredient into the glass after another until all the ingredients are in the glass. This technique is used for gin and tonics, Moscow mules, Collinses, and screwdrivers.

Layering The layering technique involves the bartender's knowledge of the specific gravity of a liquid. The heavier liquids are used as a base, while the lighter liquids are floated (or layered) on top of the heavier liquids to create a layered appearance in the glass. Examples of layered drinks include the B-52, the tequila sunrise, the black and tan, and the classic pousse-café.

Muddling The technique of muddling is highlighted by the bartender's use of a muddler to crush sugar, citrus fruit, or herbs before adding ice and alcohol to the drink. Generally, the herb or fruit should be lightly muddled as not to release bitter flavors of overmuddled items. The old-fashioned, caipirinha, mint julep, and mojito are examples of muddled drinks.

Shaking The shaking method is used for drinks that need to combine ingredients that might not easily combine in a uniform matter any other way. Shaking will also aerate the cocktail, allowing for a foam or froth on top of the cocktail. Cocktails with citrus juice or egg whites are typically shaken cocktails. Examples of cocktails that use the shaking method are the cosmopolitan, the kamikaze, and the sidecar.

Stirring Stirring is perfect for drinks that are completely made from alcoholic beverages. The purpose of stirring the drink is to make sure that you have a result that is crystal clear. To complete this technique, fill a mixing glass with ice, and then pour the ingredients into the glass. Using a barspoon, stir the drink at least forty turns or until completely chilled. Top the mixing glass with a strainer, and pour the drink into a chilled glass or a glass with ice. The Manhattan, negroni, and martini are examples of stirred cocktails.

COCKTAIL CREATION: A BALANCING ACT

Keep in mind that cocktail creation is a balancing act. A great cocktail is not too sweet, not too sour, and not too bitter. The perfect cocktail is just right. When you see a bartender stick a straw into a drink to syphon out a sip of a cocktail, the bartender is checking for balance in flavor.

A great cocktail to play with is the old-fashioned. The home bartender can play around with the recipe to see how each of the elements plays a part in the overall cocktail creation. In the case of the old-fashioned, the sugar melts into the water and provides the sweet element to the cocktail. Bitters are added to help elevate the flavor of the cocktail and to counter the sugar so that the drink is not too sweet. The spirit is added and brings the cocktail together. But wait—what type of spirit? Each spirit will have a different reaction to the overall recipe. The old-fashioned will have a different balance and different flavor based on the spirit.

Another cocktail that the home bartender can play around with is the homemade margarita. This is a splendid example of a "sour" drink. We want the margarita to be sour but not too sour, which is why we balance the drink with sweet—but not too much. This balance in flavor is important.

TWO

Cocktail Recipes

GOOD ROCK STARS LIVE LARGE—IN part because they can, but also because life is short! Alcohol lowers humans' inhibitions, which allows them to live large, at least for a little while—like a rock star! The genesis of alcoholic beverages is a near invisible process, fermentation. During fermentation, yeast converts sugar into alcohol and carbon dioxide. Fermentation creates both beer and wine. Beer is made from a liquid laced primarily with grains like barley, rice, and corn. Wine is made from the liquids from fruit. Fermented beverages like beer and wine can be served in cocktails, but they can also be distilled into spirits at a higher alcohol by volume.

Spirits fall into three categories: (1) clear spirits; (2) spirits that are sometimes clear and sometimes brown; and (3) brown spirits. Each of the spirit categories is represented in this chapter. First are the clear spirits, vodka and gin. Then are the spirits that come both clear and brown, rum and tequila (and mescal), followed by the brown spirits, brandy and whiskey. Finally, there are other cocktails that are made with wine, beer, or liqueurs. Enjoy the music and the drinks!

Vodka is the choice of bartenders. Vodka is the perfect spirit for a rock star and for a bartender, albeit for different reasons. Vodka is colorless and flavorless and has little aroma; in other words, the spirit is neutral once it is mixed into a cocktail, which allows maximum creativity from the bartender. Rock stars can mix vodka with whatever they like, or they can drink vodka straight. This lack of distinguishable character arises from distilling vodka to higher alcohol by volume and then watering it down to the desired proof. Smirnoff capitalized on this in 1953, creating an ad campaign: "It leaves you breathless!" The campaign was a play on words. But for a rock star, that is a good place to start. The vodka is undetectable when mixed with other beverages such as orange juice, tomato juice, or tonic water. Most other spirits can be detected on the breath of the person consuming that spirit.

Vodka can be made from anything, but most types are made from grains or potatoes. Today, vodka is one of the most popular spirits with bar customers. Bartenders love it too because, as many bartenders will tell you, "Vodka pays the bills."

VODKA COCKTAILS

The Beastie Boys penned a song about this cocktail on their debut album, *Licensed to Ill*, in 1986. The group consisted of Michael "Mike D" Diamond, Adam "MCA" Yauch, and Adam "Ad-Rock" Horovitz. The Beastie Boys were inducted into the Rock and Roll Hall of Fame in April 2012; less than a month later, Yauch passed away of cancer. Diamond confirmed that the Brass Monkey cocktail was something that the group enjoyed and inspired their song of the same name. Also, the term *brass monkey* is a British colloquialism for extremely cold weather, referring to it being "cold enough to freeze the balls off a brass monkey." A Brass Monkey is basically an amped-up screwdriver.

*B*RASS MONKEY

1 ounce vodka
1 ounce dark rum
1 ounce orange juice

Fill an old-fashioned glass with ice and water to chill the glass. Fill the tin side of a Boston shaker with ice. Add the vodka, dark rum, and orange juice to a mixing glass. Pour the contents of the mixing glass into the tin side of the Boston shaker and close the shaker. Shake until the ice sounds different. Empty the old-fashioned glass, then add ice. Strain the drink into the old-fashioned glass, then "put your left leg down, right leg up, tilt your head back, let's finish the cup."

In the summer of 2018, I met rock star bartender Marvin J. Allen, one of a team of talented bartenders who work at the Hotel Metropole's Carousel Bar in New Orleans. I asked him to surprise me with a drink, and he brought me a Manhattan. I am one of the many who can witness that Allen makes an incredibly delicious Manhattan! Allen is also a book author. In his book, *Magic in a Shaker: A Year of Spirited Libations*, he refers to his take on the Brass Monkey cocktail as a an amped-up Harvey Wallbanger.

*B*RASS MONKEY II

1 ½ ounces vodka
½ ounce light rum
4 ounces orange juice
½ ounce Galliano
Ice

Fill an old-fashioned glass with ice and water to chill the glass. Fill the tin side of a Boston shaker with ice. Add the vodka, light rum, and orange juice to a mixing glass. Pour the contents of the mixing glass into the tin side of the Boston shaker and close the shaker. Shake until the sound of the ice changes. Empty the old-fashioned glass, then add ice. Strain the drink into the old-fashioned glass. Float the Galliano on top of the drink.

In their 2015 debut single, the group DNCE sings about "Cake by the Ocean," which is a euphemism for *sex on the beach*. While the group makes a roundabout reference to sexual intercourse on the shore, the cocktail Sex on the Beach, created in 1987 around the same time that peach schnapps was introduced, is a direct reference to what visitors to Florida were doing on the beaches.

Sex on the Beach

1 ½ ounces vodka
1 ounce peach schnapps
1 ½ ounces cranberry juice
1 ½ ounces orange juice
1 ounce pineapple juice
Orange slice

Fill a highball glass with ice and water to chill the glass. Fill the tin side of a Boston shaker with ice. Add the vodka, peach schnapps, cranberry juice, orange juice, and pineapple juice to a mixing glass. Pour the contents of the mixing glass into the tin side of the Boston shaker and close the shaker. Shake until the sound of the ice changes. Empty the highball glass, then add ice. Strain the drink into the highball glass. Garnish with an orange slice and serve.

Gary Lewis and the Playboys hit number one with "This Diamond Ring" in 1965, cementing their place as rock stars. One of the songwriters, Alan Peter Kuperschmidt (aka Al Kooper), was a real rock star in his own right. Kooper organized the group Blood, Sweat & Tears and, as a producer, recorded Lynyrd Skynyrd's first three albums. Later, Kooper would publish a memoir, *Backstage Passes & Backstabbing Bastards: Memoirs of a Rock 'n' Roll Survivor*. Kooper has worked with many other rock stars. In 2001, the Berklee College of Music honored Kooper with an Honorary Doctorate of Music, and in 2008, he was inducted into the Musicians Hall of Fame and Museum.

Diamond Ring

1 ½ ounces vodka
1 ounce apple juice
½ ounce honey simple syrup
3 basil leaves
Apple slice

Fill a cocktail glass with ice and water to chill the glass. Fill the tin side of a Boston shaker with ice. Add the vodka, apple juice, honey simple syrup, and the basil leaves to a mixing glass. Pour the contents of the mixing glass into the tin side of the Boston shaker and close the shaker. Shake until the sound of the ice changes. Empty the cocktail glass. Strain the drink into the chilled cocktail glass. Garnish with an apple slice and serve.

Starting with a brilliant, slow, melodic guitar riff, Jimi Hendrix's "Purple Haze" adds a beating drum and then Hendrix's voice. He described "Purple Haze" as a love song, but the song evokes the psychedelic experience of the late 1960s early 1970s. Hendrix was the headliner at Woodstock, the infamous music festival. He lived the life of a rock star and died at the age of twenty-seven of a drug overdose. Hendrix's legacy is that even today he is considered one of the most influential electric guitarists in history. Hendrix was inducted into the Rock and Roll Hall of Fame in 1992.

*P*URPLE HAZE

1 ounce vodka
1 dash Cointreau
1 dash fresh lemon juice
1 dash Chambord raspberry liqueur

Prepare a shot glass. Fill the tin side of a Boston shaker with ice. Add the vodka, Cointreau, and lemon juice to a mixing glass. Pour the contents of the mixing glass into the tin side of the Boston shaker and close the shaker. Shake briefly. Strain the drink into the shot glass. Add the Chambord to the drink slowly and allow the Chambord to sink to the bottom of the glass.

Eric Clapton is the first (and the only) three-time Rock and Roll Hall of Fame inductee. He was inducted as a member of the Yardbirds (1992), Cream (1993), and as a solo artist (2000). Clapton received seventeen Grammy Awards. He is not the first rock star to covet his neighbor's (or fellow rock star's) wife, and surely he is not the last in that category. Clapton was completely smitten by model Pattie Boyd. The only problem was that Boyd was married to Beatle George Harrison. Boyd was the muse for Harrison's songs and Beatles' hits "If I Needed Someone," "Something," and "For You Blue." The conflict and yearning by Clapton led to the song "Layla." Clapton tried many things to forget Boyd, including dating Boyd's sister and getting lost in drugs and alcohol. Eventually, Harrison and Boyd divorced. Clapton and Boyd would eventually marry. Boyd is the inspiration for the song "Wonderful Tonight." Boyd must hold some record for the stimulus of so many songs.

*L*AYLA COCKTAIL

2 ounces raspberry-infused vodka
2 fresh strawberries (hulled)
2 lime wedges
4 blueberries
1 slice fresh mango
3 blueberries (for garnish)

Fill the tin side of a Boston shaker with ice. Add the lime wedges, strawberries, four blueberries, and mango slice to a mixing glass. Muddle the contents of the glass. Then add the vodka to the muddled fruit. Pour the contents of the mixing glass into the tin side of the Boston shaker and close the shaker. Shake until the sound of the ice changes. Empty the cocktail glass. Double strain the drink into the chilled cocktail glass. Garnish with three blueberries and serve.

Two songs feature Alicia Keys belting out, "Party people say, ay, it's a new day!"—one with 50 Cent rapping. Both songs are produced by Dr. Dre and Swizz Beatz. Both songs are uplifting with lyrics about overcoming hardship and starting fresh with a new day. Alicia Keys has received fifteen Grammy Awards. This is a good way to end a day or begin a new day.

**EW DAY**

1 ½ ounces vodka
½ ounce Calvados
½ ounce apricot brandy
2 ounces fresh-squeezed orange juice

Fill a sour glass or an old-fashioned glass with ice and water to chill. Fill the tin side of a Boston shaker with ice. Add the vodka, Calvados, apricot brandy, and orange juice into the glass side of the shaker, then pour the liquid into the tin and attach the two sides. Shake until the ice sounds different and the combination is cold. Discard the ice and water in the cocktail glass. Strain the cocktail into the sour glass or the old-fashioned glass. Serve.

Greta Van Fleet won Best New Artist at the 2017 Loudwire Music Awards and were nominated for four awards at the 2019 Grammys, including Best New Artist. They won the Grammy for Best Rock Album. The group was formed in 2012 in Frankenmuth, Michigan, and features three brothers, Josh, Jake, and Sam Kiszka, and drummer Danny Wagner. The group is reminiscent of Led Zeppelin. Greta Van Fleet's *From the Fires* album includes a song called "Flower Power." This cocktail is good for those who enjoy a sour drink but also like aromas of fruit and flowers.

*F*LOWER POWER SOUR

1 ½ ounces mandarin vodka
1 ounce fresh lemon juice
½ ounce mandarin brandy
¼ ounce elderflower cordial
¼ ounce simple syrup
Orange twist

Fill an old-fashioned glass with ice and water to chill. Fill the tin side of a Boston shaker with ice. Add the vodka, lemon juice, brandy, elderflower cordial, and simple syrup into the glass side of the shaker, then pour the liquid into the tin and attach the two sides. Shake until the sound of the ice changes and the combination is cold. Discard the ice and water in the old-fashioned glass then fill with ice again. Strain the cocktail into the ice-filled glass and garnish with the orange twist. Serve.

Rock stars get inspiration from many sources; the most identifiable ones are from everyday life: a lost love, how people live, an awesome event, or a special person. For the rock group Chicago, and songwriter Peter Cetera, "You're the Inspiration" was a hit in 1984 and was featured on the album *Chicago 17*. Chicago received a Grammy Award in 1976 for Best Pop Vocal Performance by a Duo, Group, or Chorus for their single "If You Leave Me Now." Chicago was inducted into the Rock and Roll Hall of Fame in 2016. This is a simple drink that looks a lot like a martini, but the addition of the Bénédictine makes this drink an inspiration!

INSPIRATION

2 ounces vodka
½ ounce dry vermouth
½ ounce Bénédictine
Lime twist

Fill a cocktail glass with ice and water to chill. Fill the tin side of a Boston shaker with ice. Add the vodka, dry vermouth, and Bénédictine into the glass side of the shaker, then pour the liquid into the tin and attach the two sides. Shake until the sound of the ice changes and the combination is cold. Discard the ice and water in the cocktail glass. Strain the cocktail into the cocktail glass and garnish with the lime twist. Serve.

The group Maroon 5 gained rock star status in 2002 with the release of their album *Songs about Jane*. The funky, jazzy album included some iconic guitar riffs by the group's lead guitarist, James Valentine. Valentine was a late addition to the group, who had already released an album under the name Kara's Flowers. The addition of Valentine seemed to complete the magic the group needed to become rock stars. This red martini is very appropriate for Valentine, who grew up in Lincoln, Nebraska (go, Big Red!), a fact that is featured in the *Songs about Jane* album cover: Valentine wearing a University of Nebraska sweatshirt while playing the guitar.

VALENTINE MARTINI

2 ounces raspberry-infused vodka
½ ounce lime juice
6 raspberries
¼ ounce simple syrup
2 raspberries (for garnish)
Lime twist

Fill a cocktail glass with ice and water to chill. Fill the tin side of a Boston shaker with ice. Add the vodka, lime juice, raspberries, and simple syrup into the glass side of the shaker. Muddle the raspberries, then pour the liquid into the tin and attach the two sides. Shake until the sound of the ice changes and the combination is cold. Discard the ice and water in the cocktail glass. Strain the cocktail into the cocktail glass and garnish with the lime twist and raspberries. Serve.

The trio of Cheryl James (Salt), Sandra Denton (Pepa), and Deidra Roper (DJ Spinderella) make up the Grammy-winning rap group Salt-N-Pepa. Groundbreakers as one of the first all-female rap groups, they are known for hits such as "Push It," "Let's Talk about Sex," "Whatta Man," "None of Your Business," and "Champagne" off of their five studio albums. This martini features the heat of pepper and flavor-enhancing salt.

SALT-N-PEPPER MARTINI

2 ounces pepper-infused vodka
½ ounce dry vermouth
Lemon wedge
Kosher salt

Fill a cocktail glass with ice and water to chill. Fill the tin side of a Boston shaker with ice. Add the vodka and dry vermouth into the glass side of the shaker, then pour the liquid into the tin and attach the two sides. Shake until the sound of the ice changes and the combination is cold. Discard the ice and water in the cocktail glass. Rub the lemon wedge on the outside rim of the glass. Dip the outside rim of the glass in the salt. Strain the cocktail into the cocktail glass. Serve.

"Calling Dr. Love" was a top-twenty hit for the iconic rock 'n' roll group KISS off their fifth studio album, *Rock and Roll Over*. KISS formed in 1973 and includes Gene Simmons, Paul Stanley, Ace Frehley, and Peter Criss in black and white face paint and distinctive stage outfits. In 2014, KISS was inducted into the Rock and Roll Hall of Fame. "Calling Dr. Love" is performed at almost every KISS concert.

THE LOVE DOCTOR

2 ounces vodka
1 ounce white crème de cacao
½ ounce raspberry liqueur

Fill a cocktail glass with ice and water to chill. Fill the tin side of a Boston shaker with ice. Add the vodka, white crème de cacao, and the raspberry liqueur into the glass side of the shaker, then pour the liquid into the tin and attach the two sides. Shake until the sound of the ice changes and the combination is cold. Discard the ice and water in the cocktail glass. Strain the cocktail into the cocktail glass. Serve.

Shelby "Sheb" Wooley is the singer/songwriter behind the song "The Purple People Eater." Wooley was also an actor featured in many westerns, including *High Noon* and *The Outlaw Josey Wales*. At one time Pat O'Brien's, the well-known New Orleans bar, featured a drink called the Purple People Eater. This cocktail is a great example of how the mixer can take over the flavor of the drink—you don't even know you are consuming alcohol.

PURPLE PEOPLE EATER

2 ounces vodka
2 ounces grape juice
1 orange slice
1 cocktail cherry

Fill a double old-fashioned glass with crushed ice. Fill the tin side of a Boston shaker with ice. Add the vodka and grape juice into the glass side of the shaker, then pour the liquid into the tin and attach the two sides. Shake until the combination is cold. Strain the cocktail into the ice-filled double old-fashioned glass and garnish with the orange slice and cocktail cherry. Serve.

Brothers Malcolm and Angus Young formed the rock 'n' roll group AC/DC in 1973 in Sydney, Australia. The group is a wonderful example of a rock group where members join and leave, but the group continues, as only Angus remains as one of the original members of the group. The group's second studio album was *T.N.T.* and featured a single by the same name. AC/DC was inducted into the Rock and Roll Hall of Fame in 2003. AC/DC won their first Grammy in 2009 for Best Hard Rock Performance for "War Machine." Pat O'Brien's in New Orleans is known for the hurricane, but at one point they also had T.N.T. on the menu.

T.N.T.

2 ounces vodka
1 ounce cranberry juice
1 ounce pineapple juice
1 orange slice
1 cocktail cherry

Fill an old-fashioned glass with crushed ice. Fill the tin side of a Boston shaker with ice. Add the vodka, cranberry juice, and pineapple juice into the glass side of the shaker, then pour the liquid into the tin and attach the two sides. Shake until the sound of the ice changes and the combination is cold. Strain the cocktail into the ice-filled old-fashioned glass and garnish with the sliced orange and cocktail cherry. Serve.

Calvin Cordozar Broadus Jr. (aka Snoop Dogg) is a talented rapper who was discovered by Dr. Dre. In 1993, Snoop Dogg's first album was released, *Doggystyle*. Dogg is known for hits such as "Gin and Juice" and "Who Am I?" but he is also known for being featured on many other artists' albums, such as Katy Perry, Dr. Dre, the Pussycat Dolls, Willie Nelson, Mariah Carey, Wiz Khalifa, Robin Thicke, and DJ Khaled, to name a few. He has been nominated for sixteen Grammy Awards but is still waiting to receive one.

OGGY STYLE

2 ounces vodka
½ ounce coffee-flavored brandy
¼ ounce cream

Fill a cocktail glass with ice and water to chill. Fill the tin side of a Boston shaker with ice. Add the vodka, coffee-flavored brandy, and cream into the glass side of the shaker, then pour the liquid into the tin and attach the two sides. Shake until the sounds of the ice changes and the combination is cold. Discard the ice and water in the cocktail glass. Strain the cocktail into the cocktail glass. Serve.

David Robert Jones (aka David Bowie) was a rock star of the highest order. One of Bowie's contributions was a character known as Major Tom. Major Tom is introduced in *Space Oddity* in 1969. Bowie and others kept us caught up with Major Tom throughout the years. The influence of the myth of Major Tom has spanned six decades. David Bowie won five Grammy Awards and was inducted into the Rock and Roll Hall of Fame 1996.

MAJOR **T**OM

1 ½ ounces vodka
½ ounce Cointreau
½ ounce kirsch
½ ounce grapefruit juice

*Fill a cocktail glass with ice and water to chill. Fill the tin
side of a Boston shaker with ice. Add the vodka, Cointreau,
kirsch, and grapefruit juice into the glass side of the shaker,
then pour the liquid into the tin and attach the two sides.
Shake until the sounds of the ice changes and the combination is cold. Discard the ice and water in the cocktail glass.
Strain the cocktail into the cocktail glass. Serve.*

"Mamma Mia," Italian for *my mother*, is a hit song from the
Swedish pop group ABBA, whose name means *father* in many
Semitic languages. ABBA formed in 1972 in Stockholm featur-
ing two male, Benny Andersson and Björn Ulvaeus, and two
female members, Anni-Frid Lyngstad and Agnetha Fältsk-
og. ABBA became one of the most commercially successful
groups of all time—rock stars! The song "Mamma Mia" was
adapted into a musical in 1999 and then into a movie in 2008.
In 2018, a sequel was released, *Mamma Mia! Here We Go Again.*
ABBA was inducted into the Rock and Roll Hall of Fame in
2010.

AMMA MIA

1 ½ ounces vodka
1 ounce amaretto
½ ounce cream

Fill a cocktail glass with ice and water to chill. Fill the tin side of a Boston shaker with ice. Add the vodka, amaretto, and cream into the glass side of the shaker, then pour the liquid into the tin and attach the two sides. Shake until the sounds of the ice changes and the combination is cold. Discard the ice and water in the cocktail glass. Strain the cocktail into the cocktail glass. Serve.

Barbara "Lady Starkey" Bach is the wife of Sir Richard Starkey, better known by his stage name, Ringo Starr, the drummer of the Beatles. Bach is also an actress and model who started enjoying fame in the 1960s. Starr married Bach in the 1980s. Bach's sister Marjorie Bach is married to rocker Joe Walsh. Starr was inducted into the Rock and Roll Hall of Fame in 1988 as a member of the Beatles and in 2015 for Music Excellence. Joe Walsh was inducted in 1998 as a member of the Eagles.

BARBARA

1 ounce vodka
1 ounce coffee liqueur
1 ounce cream
Nutmeg
Ice

Fill a cocktail glass with ice and water to chill. Fill the tin side of a Boston shaker with ice. Add the vodka, coffee liqueur, and cream into the glass side of the shaker, then pour the liquid into the tin and attach the two sides. Shake until the combination is cold. Discard the ice and water in the cocktail glass. Strain the cocktail into the cocktail glass and garnish with nutmeg. Serve.

Strawberry fields forever! John Lennon wrote the Beatles song "Strawberry Fields Forever" as an ode to a place where he enjoyed playing when he was young. The song was released in 1967 and was part of the *Sgt. Pepper's Lonely Hearts Club Band* project but was released as a single and was not part of the larger album. Lennon considered "Strawberry Fields Forever" one of his best contributions to the Beatles. The Beatles received seven Grammy Awards. John Lennon was inducted into the Rock and Roll Hall of Fame in 1988 as a member of the Beatles and in 1994 as a solo artist.

STRAWBERRY FIELDS

2 strawberries
1 ½ ounces vodka
½ ounce lime juice
½ ounce simple syrup
½ ounce egg white
Strawberry for garnish

Add ice and water to a cocktail glass to chill the glass. Add ice to the tin side of a Boston shaker. Muddle the strawberries in the bottom of the mixing glass. Add to the mixing glass simple syrup, lime juice, and vodka. Pour the contents of the mixing glass into the iced tin and secure the glass to the tin. Shake the contents until the ice sounds different and the contents are cold. Open the Boston shaker. Empty the cocktail glass, then strain the contents of the shaker into the empty glass. Garnish with a strawberry. Serve.

Gin starts as a neutral spirit, similar to vodka, but the spirit is exposed to a brand-specific proprietary mixture of seeds, roots, barks, herbs, and spices—with the most common being juniper berries. Gin remains a clear spirit. Many excellent cocktails rely on gin's specific flavor.

GIN COCKTAILS

A six-hundred-acre dairy farm in White Lake (Bethel), New York, was the site of one of the most famous rock concerts in American history: Woodstock (even though this farm is located forty-three miles to the southwest of the town that lent its name to this concert held August 15–18, 1969). The concert was billed as "3 Days of Peace & Music" and featured some of the biggest names in music, including, among others, Santana, the Grateful Dead, Creedence Clearwater Revival, Janis Joplin, the Who, Jefferson Airplane, Blood, Sweat & Tears, Joe Cocker, Jimi Hendrix, and Crosby, Stills, Nash & Young. In 2017, the National Register of Historic Places added the site of the festival to its list.

OODSTOCK

1 ounce gin
1 ounce dry vermouth
1 ounce orange juice
¼ ounce Cointreau
Orange wedge
Caster sugar
Orange twist

Fill a cocktail glass with ice and water to chill. Fill the tin side of a Boston shaker with ice. Add the gin, dry vermouth, Cointreau, and orange juice into the glass side of the shaker, then pour the liquid into the tin and attach the two sides. Shake until the ice sounds different and the combination is cold. Discard the ice and water in the cocktail glass. Rub the orange wedge on the outside rim of the glass and dip in the sugar. Strain the cocktail into the cocktail glass. Twist the orange twist over the glass, then garnish with the orange twist. Serve.

One of my favorite cocktails is the Bennett Cocktail. Similar to a gin gimlet, the Bennett Cocktail has the addition of bitters. I like to combine Angostura and Peychaud's bitters. Tony Bennett, who has had an unparalleled career, is the logical reference for this drink, but whenever I order this cocktail, I think of my brother "DJ Bennett," who wrote the "Rock Star Lexicon" for this book. He opened for many musical acts and movie openings in the Los Angeles and Southern California. He is most proud of opening for groups from New Orleans, such as Trombone Shorty and Soul Rebels.

*B*ENNETT COCKTAIL

1 ½ ounces gin
½ ounce lime juice
½ ounce simple syrup
1 dash Angostura bitters
1 dash Peychaud's bitters
Lime twist

Fill a cocktail glass with ice and water to chill. Fill the tin side of a Boston shaker with ice. Add the gin, lime juice, bitters, and simple syrup into the glass side of the shaker. Attach the two sides of the shaker. Shake until the sound of the ice changes and the combination is cold. Discard the ice and water in the cocktail glass. Strain the cocktail into the cocktail glass and garnish with the lime twist. Serve.

Anthony Ray (aka Sir Mix-a-Lot) is known for his 1992 number one hit "Baby Got Back," a song about women who have large backsides. Sir Mix-a-Lot won the 1993 Grammy Award for Best Rap Solo Performance, beating out LL Cool J, MC Hammer, Queen Latifah, and Marky Mark and the Funky Bunch, joining MC Hammer and LL Cool J as the third performer to win that category. Other performers who would eventually join this group include the who's who of rap artists, Dr. Dre, Queen Latifah, Coolio, Will Smith, Jay-Z, T.I., Kanye West, Lil Wayne, Nelly, three-time winner Miss Elliott, and four-time winner Eminem.

*T*HE BIG BOOTY

1 ounce gin
⅔ ounce lychee liqueur
½ ounce orange liqueur
½ ounce lemon juice
1 ounce papaya juice
1 slice fresh papaya

Fill a highball glass with ice to chill. Fill the tin side of a Boston shaker with ice. Add the gin, lychee liqueur, orange liqueur, lemon juice, and papaya juice into the glass side of the shaker. Attach the two sides of the shaker. Shake until the sound of the ice changes and the combination is cold. Strain the cocktail into the highball glass and garnish with a slice of fresh papaya. Serve.

Beyoncé, "Queen B," released "Single Ladies" in October 2008, and in 2010, she would win three Grammy Awards, including Song of the Year, with this quadruple-platinum hit. The Houston native sings, "Cause if you liked it, then you should have put a ring on it" in the chorus, suggesting to an ex-boyfriend that he should have made a commitment with a ring encrusted with jewels. Iconic rapper Jay-Z did put a ring on Beyoncé's hand in April 2008 before she released the song. Beyoncé has received twenty-three Grammy Awards. The Bijou is a jewel of a cocktail. The word *bijou* means jewel or trinket. This cocktail is equal parts gin, vermouth, and Chartreuse, with a dash of bitters.

IJOU

1 ounce gin
1 ounce sweet vermouth
1 ounce Chartreuse
1 dash orange bitters
Cocktail cherry
Lemon twist

Fill a cocktail glass with ice and water to chill. Fill the tin side of a Boston shaker with ice. Add the bitters, gin, sweet vermouth, and Chartreuse into the glass side of the shaker. Attach the two sides of the shaker. Shake until the sound of the ice changes and the combination is cold. Discard the ice and water in the cocktail glass. Strain the cocktail into the cocktail glass and garnish with the lemon twist and cocktail cherry. Serve.

North Carolina native Dr. Billy Taylor was a rock star jazz musician. In 1942, he graduated from Virginia State College with a degree in music. In 1975, he earned a doctorate in music education from the University of Massachusetts-Amherst. Extremely prolific, from 1951 to 2007, he produced many albums; on the face of it, he produced about one a year. During his career, he worked with many famous musicians and won many awards for his work and more than twenty honorary doctoral degrees. A teacher as well as a performer, he served as the Robert L. Jones Distinguished Professor of Music at East Carolina University in Greenville, North Carolina, and taught classes at many other institutions, including Long Island University and the Manhattan School of Music. He died of heart failure December 28, 2010, at the age of eighty-nine, and his obituary was featured in the *New York Times*.

*D*R. BILLY TAYLOR

2 ounces gin
½ ounce lime juice
4 ounces club soda
Lime twist

Fill a Collins glass with ice to chill. Fill the tin side of a Boston shaker with ice. Add the gin and lime juice into the glass side of the shaker. Attach the two sides of the shaker. Shake until the sound of the ice changes and the combination is cold. Strain the cocktail into the Collins glass, top with club soda, and garnish with the lime twist. Serve.

San Francisco serves as the inspiration for so many songs, that every person may think of a different singer or group based on individual preferences in music. Some may think of Tony Bennett and "I Left My Heart in San Francisco"; others may conjure Train's "Save Me, San Francisco" and "Half Moon Bay," Journey's "Lights," Metallica's "Battery," Jimmy

Buffet's "Come Monday," or Green Day's . . . one of their many references. Then there's Starship with "We Built This City" or the many other references from Matt Nathanson, Van Morrison, the Grateful Dead, Otis Redding, Chris Isaak, the Village People, Santana, Counting Crows, Led Zeppelin, the Bee Gees, Buddy Guy, or the many other groups who have immortalized "the city by the bay." This recipe is my version of a cocktail from the Hotel Delmano in Brooklyn, New York. As with many cocktails, the title of this recipe refers to something that is not politically correct.

*S*AN FRANCISCO HANDSHAKE

2 ounces gin (Use St. George Terroir Gin if you have it.)
1 ounce St. Germain
1 ounce lemon juice
1 dash Fernet-Branca
Sprig of thyme

Fill a cocktail glass with ice and water to chill. Fill the tin side of a Boston shaker with ice. Add the gin, St. Germain, lemon juice, and Fernet-Branca into the glass side of the shaker. Pour the liquid into the tin side and attach the two sides of the shaker. Shake until the sound of the ice changes and the combination is cold. Discard the ice and water in the cocktail glass. Strain the cocktail into the cocktail glass. Slap the thyme across the back of your hand, then garnish the drink. Serve.

In Westminster, London, England, is a famous studio, Abbey Road Studios, that since the 1930s has hosted some of the biggest names in rock, including the Beatles, Pink Floyd, Deep Purple, U2, Sting, Olivia Newton-John, Duran Duran, Wang Chung, the Alan Parsons Project, Adam Ant, the Pet Shop Boys, Genesis, Kid Rock, Chaka Khan, Maroon 5, Kanye West, Tony Bennett, and Amy Winehouse, not to mention composer John Williams of *Star Wars* and *Raiders of the Lost Ark* fame. The Beatles named their 1969 album *Abbey Road*. This cocktail is basically a gin mint julep.

*A*BBEY ROAD

2 ounces gin
1 ounce apple juice
½ ounce lemon juice
6 mint leaves
1 piece candied ginger
Lemon wheel
Mint sprig

Fill an old-fashioned glass with ice to chill. Fill the tin side of a Boston shaker with ice. Add the gin, apple juice, lemon juice, mint leaves, and candied ginger into the glass side of the shaker. Muddle the mint leaves and ginger lightly, then pour the liquid into the tin and attach the two sides. Shake until the sound of the ice changes and the combination is cold. Strain into the ice-filled old-fashioned glass. Garnish with the lemon wheel and mint sprig. Serve.

Fredrick Earl Long (aka Shorty Long) was the first to record and write, with William "Mickey" Stevenson, "Devil with a Blue Dress On" in 1964, but his version did not become a hit. A few years later, Mitch Ryder and the Detroit Wheels would hit with the same song. He wrote other songs that would become hits for other artists, including "Chantilly Lace." Long would only release two albums before he died at the age of twenty-nine, drowning after a boat crash on the Detroit River.

*D*EVIL WITH A BLUE DRESS ON

2 ounces gin
½ ounce lime juice
Splash grenadine
Splash blue curaçao
Lime twist

Fill a cocktail glass with ice and water to chill. Fill the tin side of a Boston shaker with ice. Add the gin, lime juice, grenadine, and blue curaçao into the glass side of the shaker. Pour the liquid into the tin and attach the two sides. Shake until the sound of the ice changes and the combination is cold. Discard the ice and water in the cocktail glass. Strain the cocktail into the cocktail glass and garnish with the lime twist. Serve.

What do rockers do when the band breaks up? They form a new band! There are many examples, but when Led Zeppelin decided to disband in 1980, lead singer Robert Plant formed the Honeydrippers. The band would only last from 1981 to 1985, but the members of the band included some of the who's who in the industry. For the Honeydripper's 1984 album, Jimmy Page would rejoin Plant from their days with Led Zeppelin. They were joined by Yardbird Jeff Beck and

Paul Shaffer on keyboard, as well as many others. Their soft sound included the hit "Sea of Love." Led Zeppelin was inducted into the Rock and Roll Hall of Fame in 1995.

Honey Getter

2 ounces gin
1 ounce cranberry juice
1 ounce orange juice

Fill a Collins glass with ice. Add the gin, then the cranberry juice and the orange juice. Stir. Garnish with an orange slice. Serve.

With modern technology, musical artists are discovered in many ways, including appearing on television shows such as *The Voice*, *American Idol*, and *Star Search*. Spencer Day was discovered on *Star Search*, and his smooth voice has helped launch five studio albums. Day uses his good fortune to help those less fortunate and is active promoting human rights.

Spencer Cocktail

1 ½ ounces gin
¾ ounce apricot brandy
¼ ounce orange juice
1 dash orange bitters
Lime twist

Fill a cocktail glass with ice and water to chill. Fill the tin side of a Boston shaker with ice. Add the gin, apricot brandy, orange juice, and bitters into the glass side of the shaker. Pour the liquid into the tin and attach the two sides. Shake until the sound of the ice changes and the combination is cold. Discard the ice and water in the cocktail glass. Strain the cocktail into the cocktail glass and garnish with the lime twist. Serve.

On December 6, 2014, Maroon 5 drove across Los Angeles, stopping at every wedding reception they could and filming the video for their hit song "Sugar." The video includes the confused looks of the wedding parties as the stage is being set up at the reception and the surprised looks of the brides and grooms as a curtain falls revealing Adam Levine singing and the Maroon 5 crew playing. Maroon 5 has received three Grammy Awards, including Best New Artist in 2004. This is a good drink for after the wedding.

WEDDING DAY

1 ounce gin
½ ounce vodka
1 ounce Jägermeister
4 to 5 ounces apple cider
Lime wedge
Baker's sugar

Fill a highball glass with ice. Rub the outside rim of the glass with the lime wedge, then dip the glass in the baker's sugar. Carefully add the gin, vodka, and Jägermeister. Fill the glass with apple cider. Serve.

William Michael Albert Broad (aka Billy Idol) is a punk singer who launched his career with the group Generation X. As a solo artist, he became famous with hits like "Rebel Yell," "Cradle of Love," "Dancing with Myself," and "Eyes without a Face." Idol is also known for the hit "White Wedding" off his self-titled 1982 album.

*W*HITE **W**EDDING

1 ½ ounces gin
¾ ounce peppermint liqueur

Fill a cocktail glass with ice and water to chill. Fill the tin side of a Boston shaker with ice. Add the gin and peppermint liqueur into the glass side of the shaker. Pour the liquid into the tin and attach the two sides. Shake until the sound of the ice changes and the combination is cold. Discard the ice and water in the cocktail glass. Strain the cocktail into the cocktail glass. Serve.

Moriah Rose Pereira (aka Poppy) is a multifaceted entertainer. One of her talents is singing. She released her third album in 2018, *Am I a Girl?* She also acts, has a large YouTube presence, and has authored a book.

 # *P*OPPY

1 ½ ounces dry gin
1 ounce white crème de cacao

Fill a cocktail glass with ice and water to chill. Fill the tin side of a Boston shaker with ice. Add the gin and crème de cacao into the glass side of the shaker. Pour the liquid into the tin and attach the two sides. Shake until the sound of the ice changes and the combination is cold. Discard the ice and water in the cocktail glass. Strain the cocktail into the cocktail glass. Serve.

===

Farrokh Bulsara (aka Freddie Mercury) is known for his amazing voice and was the lead singer for the rock group Queen. Many of Queen's hits feature Mercury's four-octave range that sounds similar to an opera singer. The range is showcased in "Don't Stop Me Now," "Somebody to Love," and "Bohemian Rhapsody." Mercury died in 1991 at the age of forty-five due to complications from HIV/AIDS. Queen was inducted into the Rock and Roll Hall of Fame in 2001.

*O*PERA

2 ounces of gin
1 ounce Dubonnet
½ ounce curaçao
Orange zest spiral

Add ice to a cocktail glass and a little water to chill the glass, then set the glass aside. Add the gin, Dubonnet, and curaçao. Stir until chilled (about forty stirs). Empty the cocktail glass. Add the orange spiral to the bottom and side of the glass. Strain the mixture from the mixing glass into the cocktail glass. Serve.

The gimlet is a perfect drink for a rock star: the idea is simple, but the cocktail is one of the most difficult drinks to make. There needs to be a balance between the gin, the lime, and the sweetness—just like a good band. Too much lime, and the drink will be too tart; not enough will make the drink too strong. Too much or too little sugar, and the drink will be out of balance. I suggest using sweetened lime juice to help with the formula. Tastes will vary among different palates, so you might need to experiment and adjust this drink a little.

*G*IMLET

1 ½ ounces gin
½ ounce Rose's Sweetened Lime Juice
Thin slice of lime
Ice

Fill a cocktail glass with ice and water to chill. Fill the tin side of a Boston shaker with ice. Add the gin and Rose's Sweetened Lime Juice to the glass side of the shaker, then pour the liquid into the tin and attach the two sides. Shake until the combination is cold. Discard the ice and water in the cocktail glass. Strain the gimlet into the cocktail glass, then float the lime on top. Serve.

A simple drink—gin with tonic water—but sometimes that is exactly what a rock star needs: a simple drink, easy to make and easy to drink.

*G*IN AND TONIC

2 ounces gin
4 ounces tonic water
2 slices of lime

Add ice to an old-fashioned glass. Then add the gin and top with tonic water. The carbonated tonic water will mix the drink. Garnish with lime. Serve.

The word *aviation* means all aspects of flying an aircraft. Jefferson Airplane, Jefferson Starship, and Starship are three groups that are loosely connected but refer to aviation. Some of the band members were at one point members of several of these bands. Some of the members of Jefferson Airplane continued with Jefferson Starship, and some with Jefferson Starship moved to Starship. While Jefferson Airplane is now defunct, both Jefferson Starship and Starship are both active. Jefferson Airplane was inducted into the Rock and Roll Hall of Fame in 1996.

*A*VIATION

2 ounces gin
½ ounce maraschino liqueur
½ ounce lemon juice
Cocktail cherry

Add ice and water to a cocktail glass to chill the glass. Add ice to a cocktail shaker. Add the lemon juice, maraschino liqueur, and gin to the cocktail shaker. Shake until you hear the ice change and the drink is cold. Empty the glass and strain the cocktail into the glass. Garnish with the cocktail cherry.

Every band needs a producer to help cut an album. Bernie Tom Collins (aka Tom Collins) is an award-winning producer who has won three CMA Awards for Producer of the Year. He produced Ronnie Milsap, Barbara Mandrell, and Marie Osmond, to name a few.

Tom Collins

2 ounces gin
1 ounce sour mix
4 ounces soda water
Orange slice
Cocktail cherry
Ice

Prepare a Collins glass with ice to chill the glass. Add gin and sour mix, then stir. Top with club soda and stir. Garnish with an orange slice and a cocktail cherry. Serve.

Casinos in Las Vegas have become very important for artists who don't want to tour. The artists can perform every night and then go home to have a somewhat normal homelife with their families. Concerts by Donny and Marie Osmond,

Celine Dion, Santana, Backstreet Boys, Barry Manilow, Boyz II Men, and Mariah Carey are all examples of concerts that are available.

*C*ASINO

1 ½ ounces Old Tom Gin
¼ ounce maraschino liqueur
¼ ounce orange bitters
¼ ounce lemon juice
Lemon twist
Cocktail cherry

Add ice and water to a cocktail glass to chill the glass. Add ice to the tin side of a Boston shaker. In the mixing glass, add the Old Tom Gin, maraschino liqueur, orange bitters, and lemon juice. Pour the contents of the mixing glass into the iced tin and secure the glass to the tin. Shake the contents until the ice sounds different and the contents are cold. Open the Boston shaker. Empty the cocktail glass, then strain the contents of the shaker into the empty glass. Garnish with a lemon twist and a cocktail cherry. Serve.

Peter Frampton is a legend. He has nineteen studio albums and received a Grammy Award for his 2006 album *Finger-prints*. However, his 1976 *Frampton Comes Alive* was certified eight times platinum. However, he is yet to be inducted into the Rock and Roll Hall of Fame. He is an English rose who moved to America!

ENGLISH ROSE

1 ½ ounces London Dry Gin
¾ ounce dry vermouth
¾ ounce apricot brandy
Splash of grenadine

Add ice and water to a cocktail glass to chill the glass. Add ice to the tin side of a Boston shaker. In the mixing glass, add the London Dry Gin, dry vermouth, apricot brandy, and grenadine. Pour the contents of the mixing glass into the iced tin and secure the glass to the tin. Shake the contents until the ice sounds different and the contents are cold. Open the Boston shaker. Empty the cocktail glass, then strain the contents of the shaker into the empty glass. Garnish with a lemon twist and a cocktail cherry. Serve.

At the crossroads, Robert Johnson may have made a choice. One legend says he sold his soul to the devil at the crossroads of a Mississippi highway in order to play great music. One thing is for sure, if Johnson was not the first rock 'n' roller, the blue's artist influenced the genesis of the genre. He is a member of the 27 Club. Johnson was inducted into the Rock and Roll Hall of Fame in 1986 in the first induction ceremony.

THE CROSSROADS SMASH

2 ounces dry gin
½ ounce lime juice

½ ounce simple syrup
½ ounce Cointreau
6 raspberries
6 blackberries
1 dash orange bitters
1 dash Angostura bitters
Lime wedge

Add the fruit to the bottom of and old-fashioned glass. Muddle the fruit, then add ice to an old-fashioned glass. Add ice to the tin side of a Boston shaker. In the mixing glass, add the dry gin, lime juice, simple syrup, Cointreau, and bitters. Pour the contents of the mixing glass into the iced tin and secure the glass to the tin. Shake the contents until the ice sounds different and the contents are cold. Open the Boston shaker. Strain the contents of the shaker into the empty glass. Garnish with a lime wedge. Serve.

Rum is made all over the world from sugar, sugar cane juice, molasses, or other sugar by-products. Rum is another bartender favorite because of the spirit's flexibility in cocktails. Rum comes in a wide spectrum of clear to brown colors based on how long the rum ages in oak barrels that have been burned on the inside. Most are distilled to a high proof and watered down to a market 80 proof (40 percent alcohol by volume). Some rum is sold at a higher "over-proof" 151 proof (75.5 percent alcohol by volume). Flavored rums include spiced rum, coconut rum, and rums with other fruit flavors.

RUM COCKTAILS

Barry Alan Pincus (aka Barry Manilow) has enjoyed a career that has spanned five decades. One of his hits, "Copacabana," tells the story of a showgirl, Lola, and her bartender boyfriend, Tony, both employees of the Copacabana nightclub in New York City. Tony is murdered by mobster Rico one night in a fight over Lola. The real Copacabana was at one time owned and operated by mobsters. Manilow received his only Grammy Award for Best Pop Vocal Performance, Male, for "Copacabana." This cocktail is a play on the club's name.

*C*OPABANANA

2 ounces rum
½ ounce crème de banana
½ ounce apricot brandy
1 ounce pineapple juice
1 ounce orange juice

Fill a Collins glass with ice. Pour the rum, crème de banana, apricot brandy, pineapple juice, and orange juice into the ice-filled glass. Stir. Garnish with a pineapple slice. Serve.

Lenny Kravitz is a Grammy Award–winning rock star who broke records for winning consecutive Grammy Awards in the same category, having won Best Male Rock Vocal Performance four years in a row, 1998–2001. Kravitz's mother, actress Roxie Roker, was of Bahamian ancestry. Kravitz has lived a rock star lifestyle, dating and being engaged to actresses and models while touring around the world for his craft.

*B*AHAMA MAMA

1 ½ ounces rum
1 ounce coconut rum
½ ounce cherry-flavored liqueur
½ ounce lemon juice
2 ounces orange juice
2 ounces pineapple juice
Splash of grenadine
Orange slice
Cocktail cherry

Fill a hurricane glass or a highball with ice. Add the rum, coconut rum, cherry-flavored liqueur, lemon juice, orange juice, and pineapple juice to a cocktail glass. Roll the liquid from one cocktail glass to another filled with ice. Roll the drink back and forth between the glasses. Strain the cocktail into the prepared glass and top with grenadine. Garnish with an orange slice and a cherry. Serve.

During a Carpool Karaoke segment on *The Late Late Show with James Corden*, Corden asked Rod Stewart, "What is the most rock-and-roll experience of your life?" Stewart responded, "Oh, I don't know, there have been so many . . . drinking and shagging, drinking and shagging." Stewart started performing with various groups in the 1960s but established a solo career in 1969 and is still active today. Stewart is known for his affairs with women, fathering eight children by five mothers. Many of his affairs were with models or actresses. Rod Stewart received a Grammy in 2004 for Best Traditional Pop Vocal Album and was inducted into the Rock and Roll Hall of Fame in 1994 for his solo career and again in 2012 for his contribution, as lead singer, to the Small Faces.

*B*ETWEEN THE SHEETS

1 ounce rum
1 ounce brandy
1 ounce triple sec

Fill a cocktail glass with ice and water to chill. Fill the tin side of a Boston shaker with ice. Add the rum, brandy, and triple sec into the glass side of the shaker. Pour the liquid into the tin and attach the two sides. Shake until the sound of the ice changes and the combination is cold. Discard the ice and water in the cocktail glass. Strain the cocktail into the cocktail glass. Serve.

Mental illness is nothing to make fun of; many have described the illness as a cranial meltdown. Few would think this was an appropriate theme for a song, but the Counting Crows hit with "Round Here" on their debut album. Counting Crows lead singer Adam Duritz bravely discussed his own struggles with mental illness in 2008 in an autobiographical article in *Men's Health*. He discussed triggers that happened during the band's first Australian tour and how he worked with doctors to manage his condition.

CRANIAL MELTDOWN

1 ½ ounces rum

1 ½ ounces coconut rum

1 ½ ounces raspberry liqueur

Fill a highball glass with ice. Fill the tin side of a Boston shaker with ice. Add the rum, coconut rum, and raspberry liqueur into the glass side of the shaker. Pour the liquid into the tin and attach the two sides. Shake until the sound of the ice changes and the combination is cold. Strain the cocktail into the ice-filled highball glass. Serve.

In 1968, John Lennon and Yoko Ono caused a stir with their album *Unfinished Music No. 1: Two Virgins* without anyone ever having listened to the music. The cover of the album featured the two artists without clothes. The two would eventually marry and have a son, Sean. Lennon received seven Grammy Awards. Lennon was inducted into the Rock and Roll Hall of Fame twice, in 1988 as a member of the Beatles and in 1994 as a solo artist.

GETTING NAKED

1 ounce rum
1 ounce peach schnapps
1 ounce blue curaçao

Fill an old-fashioned glass with ice. Fill the tin side of a Boston shaker with ice. Add the rum, peach schnapps, and blue curaçao into the glass side of the shaker. Pour the liquid into the tin and attach the two sides. Shake until the sound of the ice changes and the combination is cold. Strain the cocktail into the ice-filled old-fashioned glass. Serve.

Robert K. McFerrin Jr. (aka Bobby McFerrin) is a ten-time Grammy Award winner. McFerrin's 1988 hit "Don't Worry Be Happy" won both Song of the Year and Record of the Year at the 1989 Grammy Awards. The song was the first a cappella song to reach number one on the Billboard Hot 100 chart. The song was featured in the 1988 film *Cocktail*, starring Tom Cruise, Elisabeth Shue, and Bryan Brown. The song is played as Cruise's character, Brian Flanagan, meets Shue's Jordon Mooney in Jamaica where Flanagan is a bartender. Doug Coughlin, played by Brown, enters back into the story and reacquaints himself with Flanagan. McFerrin has received ten Grammy Awards.

JAMAICAN TEA

1 ounce dark rum
1 ounce triple sec
2 ounces sour mix
1 ounce cola
Lemon slice

Fill a highball glass with ice. Pour the rum, triple sec, sour mix into the glass, then stir. Top with cola and garnish with the lemon slice. Serve.

Sixpence None the Richer is a Christian rock band that had a popular crossover hit—"Kiss Me"—in 1998. The Grammy Award–nominated group from New Braunfels, Texas, produced an international hit, which would be one of many songs that would be used on a "kiss cam" at sporting events.

JUMP UP AND KISS ME

1 ounce rum
1 ounce Galliano
1 ounce apricot brandy
4 ounces pineapple juice
Splash of grenadine

Fill a small beer mug (12 ounces) with ice. Add the rum, Galliano, apricot brandy, and pineapple juice to the beer mug. Stir. Float the grenadine on top of the drink. Serve.

Painkiller was a band in the 1990s that included John Zorn on saxophone, Bill Laswell on bass guitar, and Mick Harris on drums. The trio produced four albums in five years. Harris left the band in 1995, but the group reformed to include other members.

PAINKILLER

1 ½ ounces rum
3 ounces orange juice
3 ounces pineapple juice
½ ounce Coco López
Dash of nutmeg

Fill a highball glass with ice. Fill the tin side of a Boston shaker with ice. Add the rum, orange juice, pineapple juice, and Coco López into the glass side of the shaker. Pour the liquid into the tin and attach the two sides. Shake until the sound of the ice changes and the combination is cold. Strain the cocktail into the ice-filled highball glass and garnish with the nutmeg. Serve.

British rapper SNE paired up with Footsteps for the song "Rum Punch," a catchy tune with Caribbean influence. Rum punch is easy to make and is very tasty too. Remember this rhyme: one part sour, two parts sweet, three parts rum, four parts weak. Perhaps that is why it is popular.

UM PUNCH

½ ounce lemon or lime juice
1 ounce simple syrup
1 ½ ounces rum
2 ounces water

Fill an old-fashioned glass with ice. Fill the tin side of a Boston shaker with ice. Add the lemon or lime juice, simple syrup, rum, and water into the glass side of the shaker. Pour the liquid into the tin and attach the two sides. Shake until the sound of the ice changes and the combination is cold. Strain the cocktail into the ice-filled old-fashioned glass. Serve.

Phillip David Charles Collins (aka Phil Collins) is a British drummer and vocalist. He started as the drummer for Genesis in 1970 and moved to lead singer in 1975 when Peter Gabriel left for a solo career. Later Collins also enjoyed a solo career. His accolades include an Academy Award, eight Grammy Awards, and induction in several hall of fames, including the Rock and Roll Hall of Fame in 2010 as a member of Genesis.

Rum Ta Tum

1 ounce rum
1 ounce cherry juice
1 ounce lemonade
1 ounce pineapple juice

Fill a highball glass with ice and water to chill. Fill the tin side of a Boston shaker with ice. Add the rum, cherry juice, lemonade, and pineapple juice into the glass side of the shaker. Pour the liquid into the tin and attach the two sides. Shake until the sound of the ice changes and the combination is cold. Strain the cocktail into the ice-filled highball glass. Serve.

Train has ten studio albums to their credit, with eight Grammy nominations and three wins. Their hits include "Meet Virginia," "Drops of Jupiter," "Hey, Soul Sister," "Marry Me," and "Save Me, San Francisco." Train's front man, Patrick Monahan, is backed up by six others, including Hector Maldonado, Luis Maldonado, Jerry Becker, Drew Shoals, Nikita Houston, and Sakai Smith. Train received the Grammy Award for Best Pop Performance by a Duo or Group with Vocals for "Hey, Soul Sister in 2010."

Runaway Train

1 ounce rum
1 ounce triple sec

1 ounce sour mix
1 ounce grapefruit juice
1 ounce cola
Grapefruit wedge

Fill a highball glass with ice. Add the rum, triple sec, sour mix, grapefruit juice, and cola. Garnish with a grapefruit wedge. Serve.

Jack Johnson was born in Hawaii, so music and surfing are in his blood. He learned to surf and play the guitar before the age of ten. He was a professional surfer before starting a successful singing career. Much of his music is influenced by surfing or by the surfing lifestyle. His comfort with the water is featured in many of his videos—seemingly always near a beach or in the water.

$\mathcal{S}$URFER MARTINI

1 ounce rum
½ ounce coconut rum
½ ounce banana liqueur
1 ounce pineapple juice

Fill a cocktail glass with ice and water to chill. Fill the tin side of a Boston shaker with ice. Add the rum, coconut rum, banana liqueur, and pineapple juice into the glass side of the shaker. Pour the liquid into the tin and attach the two sides. Shake until the sound of the ice changes and the combination is cold. Discard the ice and water in the cocktail glass. Strain the cocktail into the cocktail glass. Serve.

Jamaican singer Robert Nesta Marley (aka Bob Marley) was the front man for the Wailers, a group that included Winston Hubert McIntosh (aka Peter Tosh) and Neville O'Riley Livingston (aka Bunny Wailer), among others. They had many hits on their thirteen albums (which they created in eighteen years), including "Jamming," "Simmer Down," "Judge Not," "Get Up, Stand Up," "I Shot the Sheriff," and "Three Little Birds," to name a few. During the 1980s, Marley passed away from cancer, and Tosh was assassinated during a home invasion. Their song "Wake Up and Live" discusses taking advantage of today and making dreams reality. Bob Marley was inducted into the Rock and Roll Hall of Fame in 1994.

CARPE DIEM

1 ½ ounces high-proof rum
Splash blue curaçao
Splash mescal
½ ounce lemon juice
1 ounce passion fruit juice

Fill a cocktail glass with ice and water to chill. Fill the tin side of a Boston shaker with ice. Add the rum, blue curaçao, mescal, lemon juice, and passion fruit juice into the glass side of the shaker. Pour the liquid into the tin and attach the two sides. Shake until the sound of the ice changes and the combination is cold. Discard the ice and water in the cocktail glass. Strain the cocktail into the cocktail glass. Serve.

If you are trying to look like a rock star, consider making this drink—perhaps you will look like a rock star. Remember that being a rock star is hard work because for many, the rocking is a side job. Dr. Phil hosted a wannabe rock star on his show who was too busy trying to be a rock star to have a job. Dr. Phil asked Gene Simmons to provide some advice to the future rock star. The KISS front man nicely said, "Get a damn job!"

Rock Star

¼ ounce 151-proof rum
¼ ounce Jägermeister
¼ ounce triple sec
¼ ounce sloe gin
¼ ounce cinnamon schnapps

Fill a shot glass with each of the liquors and liqueurs. Serve.

The Canadian rock group Barenaked Ladies is known for their fun, comedic ballads that sometimes include a rap-style performance. Examples of their style is "Another Postcard" and "If I Had a Million Dollars." The group was already famous when they wrote the theme song for the television show *The Big Bang Theory*.

*B*ARE NAKED LADY

1 ounce dark rum
1 ounce apple brandy
3 ounces sour mix
2 ounces orange juice
Orange slice

Fill a highball glass with ice. Add the rum, brandy, sour mix, and orange juice. Stir, garnish with an orange slice, and serve.

The Go-Go's were the first all-female group to have a number one album in the United States in part because of the distinctive voice of lead singer Belinda Carlisle. The Go-Go's started in the punk scene of Los Angeles but quickly moved mainstream. They had hits that included "Our Lips Are Sealed," "We Got the Beat," and "Vacation." Carlisle would have a solo career but would come back to the group.

*B*ELINDA

1 ½ ounces dark rum
¾ ounce dry vermouth
¼ ounce crème de banana
¼ ounce amaretto

Fill a cocktail glass with ice and water to chill. Fill the tin side of a Boston shaker with ice. Add the dark rum, dry vermouth, crème de banana, and amaretto into the glass side of the shaker. Pour the liquid into the tin and attach the two sides. Shake until the sound of the ice changes and the combination is cold. Discard the ice and water in the cocktail glass. Strain the cocktail into the cocktail glass. Serve.

Anthony T. Smith (aka Tone Loc) is a Grammy-nominated rap artist who is known for his songs "Wild Thing" and "Funky Cold Medina." Based in Los Angeles, he has produced two albums.

ILD THANG

½ ounce rum
½ ounce dark rum
½ ounce gin
½ ounce triple sec
½ ounce maraschino liqueur
½ ounce papaya juice
1 ounce pineapple juice
1 ounce orange juice
Splash 151-proof rum

Fill a hurricane glass with ice. Add the rum, dark rum, gin, triple sec, maraschino liqueur, papaya juice, pineapple juice, and orange juice into the ice-filled glass. Float the 151-rum on top. Serve.

"Love Shack" was the summer hit in 1989 for the B-52's and helped facilitate a comeback for the group. The cabin, located near Athens, Georgia, that served as the inspiration for the song burned down in 2004. Kate Pierson, the band's keyboardist and vocalist, lived in the house in the 1970s.

*L*OVE SHACK

1 ½ ounces dark rum
1 ounce orange juice
4 to 5 ounces lemon-lime soda
Splash of grenadine

Fill a Collins glass with ice. Add the rum, orange juice, and lemon-lime soda and top with grenadine. Stir and serve.

Astrud Gilberto is a bossa nova singer who is known worldwide for "The Girl from Ipanema," which won Record of the Year at the 1965 Grammy Awards. Gilberto, who is from Brazil, would go on to record sixteen studio albums, sixteen compilation albums, and two live albums.

*B*OSSA NOVA

2 ounces white rum
½ ounce Galliano
½ ounce apricot brandy
4 ounces apple juice
1 ounce lime juice
½ ounce simple syrup

Lime wheel or lime wedge
Ice

Add ice and water to a highball glass to chill the glass. Add ice to the tin side of a Boston shaker. In the mixing glass, add the rum, Galliano, apricot brandy, apple juice, lime juice, and simple syrup. Pour the contents of the mixing glass into the iced tin and secure the glass to the tin. Shake the contents until the ice sounds different and the contents are cold. Open the Boston shaker. Empty the highball glass, refill with ice, and then strain the contents of the shaker into the glass. Garnish with a lime wheel or wedge. Serve.

Jean-Philip Grobler is the lead singer for his group St. Lucia. Originally from South Africa, he now lives in Brooklyn, New York. Since 2012, the group has released three albums. There are rumors that the third album, *Hyperion*, may be the last offering from the group, which includes Ross Clark on bass guitar, Nick Paul on keyboard, Dustin Kaufman on drums, and Patti Beranek on keyboard and backing vocals.

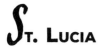T. LUCIA

2 ounces rum (white or golden)
1 ounce dry vermouth
1 ounce triple sec or curaçao
2 ounces orange juice
1 teaspoon grenadine
Cocktail cherry
Orange twist

Add ice and water to a highball glass to chill the glass. Add ice to the tin side of a Boston shaker. In the mixing glass, add the rum, vermouth, triple sec or curaçao, orange juice, and grenadine. Pour the contents of the mixing glass into the iced tin and secure the glass to the tin. Shake the contents until the ice sounds different and the contents are cold. Open the Boston shaker. Empty the highball glass, refill with ice, and then strain the contents of the shaker into the glass. Garnish with the orange twist and cocktail cherry. Serve.

Tequila and mescal are both made from the agave plant. The agave plant takes between eight to twelve years to reach maturity, which means tequila makers must project a decade in advance the demand for tequila. Like rum, tequila is aged to varying degrees in burned oak barrels, many of them used bourbon and Cognac barrels. As the tequila ages, the charred barrels lend more color to the spirit. Blanco or plata is tequila that is aged less than two months in stainless steel or neutral oak barrels. Joven or oro is generally unaged tequila that is flavored with caramel coloring. Reposado is tequila that is aged in oak barrels a minimum of two months but less than a year. Añejo is tequila that is aged in oak barrels for a minimum of a year but less than three years. Finally, extra añejo is aged in oak barrels for a minimum of three years. The longer that tequila is aged, the darker the liquid becomes and the more influence the wood has on the flavor. The longer that tequila is aged, the higher the price of the tequila. Cocktails rarely call for the pricy, long-aged tequilas.

TEQUILA AND MESCAL COCKTAILS

Jimmy Buffett not only wrote and sang the quintessential song about a drink but built an empire on that drink, the margarita. Today, most major cities have a Margaritaville restaurant, but that is just the tip of the sandbar. Buffett owns Margaritaville Tequila, Margaritaville Food, Margaritaville Footwear, and Margaritaville Records. He has a beer produced by Anheuser-Busch called LandShark Lager and a retirement village in Daytona Beach, Florida, called Latitude Margaritaville. Buffett may not have set out to be a rock star, but his music stood the test of time and found several generations who related with his message. Many of Buffett's songs incorporate a tropical theme, and many are about drinking and relaxation. If you enjoy this one too much, hell, it could be your fault.

MARGARITA

2 ounces tequila
1 ounce lime juice
1 ounce Cointreau
1 lime wheel (for garnish)
1 lime wedge
Kosher salt

First search for your lost shaker of salt . . . Fill a margarita or cocktail glass with ice and water to chill the glass. Fill the tin side of a Boston shaker with ice. Add the tequila, lime juice, and Cointreau to a mixing glass. Pour the contents of the mixing glass into the tin side of the Boston shaker and close the shaker. Shake until the sound of the ice changes.

Empty the margarita or cocktail glass. Rub the edge of the glass with the lime wedge and then dip the edge into the salt. Strain the drink into the margarita or cocktail glass. Garnish with the lime wheel and serve.

Herbert Alpert (aka Herb Alpert) is many things: a record producer, record executive, songwriter, trumpeter, singer, and Grammy Award winner with multiple gold and platinum records. Alpert created a studio in his garage to record the first record of Herb Alpert and the Tijuana Brass. This was A&M Records' first release. A&M stands for Alpert and (Jerry) Moss. They recorded many acts, including Burt Bacharach, Sérgio Mendes, the Carpenters, Captain and Tennille, and Quincy Jones. Alpert has received eight Grammy Awards. His first was in 1965, and his most recent was in 2013. Both Alpert and Jerry Moss were inducted into the Rock and Roll Hall of Fame in 2006.

*B*RASS

2 ounces tequila
2 ounces passion fruit liqueur

Fill a double old-fashioned glass with ice. Add the tequila and then the passion fruit liqueur to the ice-filled glass. Stir. Serve.

Stefani Joanne Angelina Germanotta (aka Lady Gaga) is a complicated, multifaceted lady. A singer/songwriter, an actress, and an activist, Gaga has won nine Grammy Awards, two Golden Globes, and the 2019 Academy Award for the song "Shallow," from *A Star Is Born*, an award she shared with Mark Ronson, Andrew Wyatt, and Anthony Rossomando. She and costar Bradley Cooper crushed their Oscars performance. Lady Gaga was also nominated for Best Actress for the same role.

COMPLICATED LADY

1 ounce tequila
½ ounce apricot brandy
½ ounce Cointreau
1 ounce lime juice
½ ounce egg white
Lime twist

Fill a cocktail glass with ice and water to chill. Fill the tin side of a Boston shaker with ice. Add the tequila, apricot brandy, Cointreau, lime juice, and egg white into the glass side of the shaker. Pour the liquid into the tin and attach the two sides. Shake until the sound of the ice changes and the combination is cold. Discard the ice and water in the cocktail glass. Strain the cocktail into the cocktail glass and garnish with the lime twist. Serve.

Sammy Hagar was already a rock star with solo hits like "I Can't Drive 55" when he joined Van Halen. With Van Halen, Hagar hit new heights—the nickname for the band at this time was "Van Hagar." Later, he would own Cabo Wabo Tequila and Sammy's Beach Bar Rum. The only Grammy Award Hager has received was for his work with Van Halen in 1991 for Best Hard Rock Performance with Vocals for *For Unlawful Carnal Knowledge*. Van Halen was inducted into the Rock and Roll Hall of Fame in 2007.

*C*ABO

1 ½ ounces tequila
1 ½ ounces pineapple juice
½ ounce lime juice
Lime twist

Fill a cocktail glass with ice and water to chill. Fill the tin side of a Boston shaker with ice. Add the tequila, pineapple juice, and lime juice into the glass side of the shaker. Pour the liquid into the tin and attach the two sides. Shake until the sound of the ice changes and the combination is cold. Discard the ice and water in the cocktail glass. Strain the cocktail into the cocktail glass and garnish with the lime twist. Serve.

Katheryn Elizabeth Hudson (aka Katy Perry) found rock stardom 2010 with her third album, *Teenage Dream*. She was only the second artist in the United States to produce an album with five number one hits (the first was Michael Jackson's *Bad*). Perry has won many awards. However, even with all her success and thirteen nominations, she has never won a Grammy Award. In 2018, Perry joined the revival of *American Idol* as a judge.

*C*ALIFORNIA **D**REAM

2 ounces tequila
1 ounce sweet vermouth
½ ounce dry vermouth
Lemon twist
Orange twist

Fill a cocktail glass with ice and water to chill. Fill the tin side of a Boston shaker with ice. Add the tequila, sweet vermouth, and dry vermouth into the glass side of the shaker. Pour the liquid into the tin and attach the two sides. Shake until the sound of the ice changes and the combination is cold. Discard the ice and water in the cocktail glass. Strain the cocktail into the cocktail glass, express the oil from the lemon twist, discard the lemon twist, and garnish with the orange twist. Serve.

California rockers the Beach Boys sing about typical high school interests: girls, cars, and surfing. The band originally consisted of three brothers, Brian, Carl, and Dennis Wilson, cousin Mike Love, and friend Al Jardine. Their 1966 hit "Good Vibrations" is an iconic sample of their work. The Beach Boys were inducted into the Rock and Roll Hall of Fame in 1988.

Good Vibrations

2 ounces tequila
2 ounces orange juice
Lime twist

Fill an old-fashioned glass with ice. Add the tequila and the orange juice. Stir. Garnish with the lime twist. Serve.

The pink Cadillac has played an important role in American music. Both Aretha Franklin, the Queen of Soul, and Natalie Cole have sung about this iconic car. Franklin, winner of eighteen Grammy Awards and recipient of the Presidential Medal of Freedom and at least twelve honorary doctoral degrees, has the distinction of being the first woman to be inducted into the Rock and Roll Hall of Fame in 1987. Franklin released "Freeway of Love (In a Pink Cadillac)" in 1985, for which she would win a Grammy. The song and video features saxophonist Clarence Clemons, who was a member of Bruce Springsteen's E Street Band. Natalie Cole covered Bruce Springsteen's "Pink Cadillac" in 1987. Cole won a total of seven Grammy Awards.

Pink Cadillac Margarita

1 ounce tequila
½ ounce triple sec
1 ounce lime juice
½ ounce cranberry juice

½ ounce simple syrup
Lime twist

Fill a cocktail glass with ice and water to chill. Fill the tin side of a Boston shaker with ice. Add the tequila, triple sec, lime juice, cranberry juice, and simple syrup into the glass side of the shaker. Pour the liquid into the tin and attach the two sides. Shake until the sound of the ice changes and the combination is cold. Discard the ice and water in the cocktail glass. Strain the cocktail into the cocktail glass and garnish with the lime twist. Serve.

Trumpeter Miles Davis teamed up with bass guitarist William Henry Marcus Miller Jr. (aka Marcus Miller) for the jazz album *Music from Siesta*, which has a Spanish influence. A *siesta* is a midafternoon nap. A siesta is a good idea for a rock star, so he or she can rock all night long. Miller has received two Grammy Awards. Davis received eight Grammy Awards and was inducted into the Rock and Roll Hall of Fame in 2006.

SIESTA

1 ½ ounces tequila
¾ ounce lime juice
½ ounce sloe gin

Fill a cocktail glass with ice and water to chill. Fill the tin side of a Boston shaker with ice. Add the tequila, lime juice, and sloe gin into the glass side of the shaker. Pour the liquid into the tin and attach the two sides. Shake until the sound of the ice changes and the combination is cold. Discard the ice and water in the cocktail glass. Strain the cocktail into the cocktail glass. Serve.

ZZ Top is a three-man rock band from Houston, Texas, including Billy Gibbons, Frank Beard, and Dusty Hill. ZZ Top has fifteen studio albums (some gold, some platinum, and one diamond) and are known for songs like "Legs" and "Sharp Dressed Man." The band was inducted into the Rock and Roll Hall of Fame in 2004.

*L*EGS

¾ ounce tequila
¾ ounce Jägermeister
1 dash Tabasco sauce

Pour the tequila and Jägermeister into a shot glass. Top with Tabasco sauce. Serve.

Gordon Sumner (aka Sting) was the lead singer and bassist for the group the Police. Sting was joined by British guitarist Andy Summers and American drummer Stewart Copeland to form the Police, a group that would win five Grammy Awards on five studio albums before Sting quit the group for a solo career. Sting wrote the majority of the Police's songs. Sting has received seventeen Grammy Awards. The Police were inducted into the Rock and Roll Hall of Fame in 2003.

*B*AD **STING**

½ ounce grenadine
½ ounce pastis
½ ounce Cointreau
½ ounce tequila

Add grenadine to a shot glass. Insert a spoon curve side up and carefully pour the pastis on the back of the spoon, allowing the liqueur to layer on top of the grenadine. Repeat with the Cointreau and the tequila. Serve.

The Crash Test Dummies are a rock group from Canada known for their song, "Mmm Mmm Mmm Mmm" and "Superman's Song." Front man Brad Roberts has a distinctively low voice, which helps distinguish the group from other groups.

*C*RASH **TEST** **DUMMY** **SHOTS**

½ ounce tequila
½ ounce triple sec
1 ounce sour mix

Put a shot glass on the bar. Fill the tin side of a Boston shaker with ice. Add the tequila, triple sec, and sour mix into the glass side of the shaker. Pour the liquid into the tin and attach the two sides. Shake until the sound of the ice changes and the combination is cold. Strain the cocktail into the shot glass. Serve.

The Troggs are an English rock band known for the song "Wild Thing." However, the song was written by American James Voight (aka Chip Taylor), the brother of actor John Voight. Taylor wrote many other songs that were covered by Janis Joplin, Jimi Hendrix, and Ace Frehley, to name a few.

WILD THING

1 ½ ounces tequila
1 ounce cranberry juice
1 ounce club soda
½ ounce lime juice
Lime twist

Fill an old-fashioned glass with ice. Add the tequila, cranberry juice, lime juice, and club soda. Garnish with a lime twist. Serve.

Richard Valenzuela (aka Ritchie Valens) was already a rock star when he died at age seventeen with fellow rockers Charles Holley (aka Buddy Holly) and J. P. Richardson Jr. (aka the Big Bopper) on February 3, 1959. Don McLean refers to the day as "the day the music died" in his hit "American Pie." Valens was known for his song "La Bamba," a single released in 1958. Ritchie Valens was inducted into the Rock and Roll Hall of Fame in 2001.

A BAMBA

1 ½ ounces tequila

¾ ounce Cointreau

1 ounce pineapple juice

1 ounce orange juice

Splash of grenadine

Orange slice

Cocktail cherry

Fill a Collins glass with ice. Add the tequila, Cointreau, pine-apple juice, and orange juice. Top with a splash of grenadine. Garnish with an orange slice and cocktail cherry. Serve.

British brothers Barry, Robin, and Maurice Gibb formed the Bee Gees in 1958 and are perhaps best known for their music in the late 1960s and 1970s, including their work on the soundtrack for the movie *Saturday Night Fever*. John Travolta danced to their music in the movie. The Bee Gees received five Grammy Awards and were inducted into the Rock and Roll Hall of Fame in 1997.

*S*ATURDAY NIGHT FEVER

1 ½ ounces reposado tequila

1 ounce passion fruit liqueur

⅔ ounce kiwi schnapps

2 ounces cream

2 ounces melon puree

1 cup ice

Fill a blender with ice, tequila, passion fruit liqueur, kiwi schnapps, cream, and melon puree. Blend until smooth. Pour into a Collins glass. Serve.

The song starts with a single guitar riff: the Kinks' "Lola"— "Lo-lo-lo-lo-Lola"—the song about a transvestite who the singer meets in a club in Soho. They "drank champagne and danced all night," during which he notices that "she walked like a woman but talked like a man." He almost falls for Lola, but he pushes her away and walks off. The song ends with the listener speculating what happened between the singer and Lola. The Kinks were inducted into the Rock and Roll Hall of Fame in 1990.

*H*ER NAME WAS LOLA

1 ½ ounces tequila
1 ounce lime juice
½ ounce honey simple syrup
½ ounce Cointreau
Orange twist

Fill a cocktail glass with ice and water to chill. Fill the tin side of a Boston shaker with ice. Add the tequila, lime juice, honey simple syrup, and Cointreau into the glass side of the shaker. Pour the liquid into the tin and attach the two sides. Shake until the sound of the ice changes and the combination is cold. Discard the ice and water in the cocktail glass. Strain the cocktail into the cocktail glass and garnish with the orange twist. Serve.

Alecia Beth Moore (aka P!nk) has three Grammy Awards and an Emmy Award as some of the many accolades during her career. Her distinctive voice highlights songs like, "So What," "Get the Party Started," and "Raise Your Glass." In "So What," she discusses her rock star status. She wants to start a fight because her husband left. But she sings, "So, so what? I'm still a rock star. I got my rock moves and I don't need you. And guess what I'm having more fun and now that we're done I'm going to show you tonight, I'm alright . . ." as the video clearly shows her upset. P!nk has received three Grammy Awards.

!NK PALOMA

2 ounces tequila
3 ounces Texas ruby red grapefruit juice
3 ounces sparkling water
Lime wedge
Kosher salt

Rub the lime wedge around the edge of the outside of a highball glass and dip the glass into the salt. Fill the highball glass with ice. Fill the tin side of a Boston shaker with ice. Add the tequila and grapefruit juice into the glass side of the shaker. Pour the liquid into the tin and attach the two sides. Shake until the sound of the ice changes and the combination is cold. Strain the cocktail into the highball glass, top with sparkling water, and garnish with the lime wedge. Serve.

Every night leads to a sunrise. If you are going to start the morning with a drink, consider the Tequila Sunrise. The Eagles recorded their song "Tequila Sunrise" in 1973 for the *Desperado* album. The song hit the charts in 1975. The song was written by Don Henley and Glenn Frey. The Eagles received six Grammy Awards and were inducted into the Rock and Roll Hall of Fame in 1998.

Tequila Sunrise

1 ½ ounces tequila
3 ounces orange juice
½ ounce grenadine syrup
Orange slice
Cocktail cherry

Add ice to an old-fashioned glass to chill the glass. Add tequila and orange juice. Add the grenadine, which will sink to the bottom of the glass, then stir gently. Serve.

Brandy is distilled wine. Most brandy has a golden hue from barrel aging; however, some brandy is clear because either the barrels were old and used with no color left to lend to the brandy or the brandy was not aged at all. Cognac, Armagnac, and Calvados are three examples of famous French brandy. Cognac is distilled from a wine made from a mixture of mostly Ugni Blanc (Trebbiano) and to a lesser extent Folle Blanche and Colombard. Cognac comes from the Cognac region just north of Bordeaux. Armagnac starts as grape wine from ten different grapes but mostly the same grapes used to make Cognac. Armagnac is produced in the Armagnac region in Gascony in Southwest France. Calvados begins as apple wine in the northern Normandy region of France. The longer brandy is aged, the higher the price. For cocktails, you may consider using younger product unless you are trying to make a statement—but know that the subtle differences that are clear to the palate are lost in the mixture of a cocktail. Brandy is also made in the Americas, with examples from both

North and South America. Cognac, Armagnac, and Calvados are all considered luxury products, which is why they would be the product of choice of a rock star, especially one with a seemingly unlimited expense account. For those rock stars on a limited expense accounts, there are excellent substitutes at lower price points.

BRANDY COCKTAILS

Daryl Hohl (aka Daryl Hall) and John Oates are an American rock 'n' roll duo. In 1982, they released the Billboard number one single "Maneater" off their eleventh studio album *H2O*. To date they have eighteen albums. In 2007, Hall started a live broadcast from his house in Pawling, New York, that over the years has included many rock stars. Many clips are available on YouTube. Hall and Oates were inducted into the Rock and Roll Hall of Fame in 2014.

MAN EATER

1 ½ ounces brandy
½ ounce Southern Comfort
1 dash orange bitters

Fill a cocktail glass with ice and water to chill. Fill the tin side of a Boston shaker with ice. Add the brandy, Southern Comfort, and orange bitters into the glass side of the shaker, then pour the liquid into the tin and attach the two sides. Shake until the sounds of the ice changes and the combination is cold. Discard the ice and water in the cocktail glass. Strain the cocktail into the cocktail glass. Serve.

Norman Jeffery Healey (aka Jeff Healey) was a guitarist and singer/songwriter who is known for the hit "Angel Eyes." Extremely talented on the guitar, Healey learned to play early even though he lost his sight due to a rare form a cancer. He would pass away in 2008 of cancer.

*A*NGEL WING

1 ounce white crème de cacao
1 ounce brandy
¼ ounce light cream

Add the white crème de cacao to a shot glass. Flip a spoon upside down so the curved side is facing up. Put the spoon against the side of the shot glass. Carefully pour the brandy on top of the spoon. The brandy should layer on top of the crème de cacao. Repeat with the cream. Serve.

Robin Thicke has seven studio albums to his credit and several international hits, including "Blurred Lines." Thicke joined with Jay-Z for "Meiplé" off his *Sex Therapy* album. He clearly sings about a trip to Paris with his wife, actress Paula Patton. Thicke has worked with many other artists, including Snoop Dogg, Nicki Minaj, and Pharrell Williams. His divorce with Patton came on the heels of "Blurred Lines" and created a public relations nightmare for Thicke during a period of time when he lost his father, actor Alan Thicke.

*C*HAMPS ELYSEES COCKTAIL

1 ½ ounces brandy
¾ ounce Yellow Chartreuse
¼ ounce lemon juice
¼ ounce simple syrup
1 dash Angostura bitters
Lemon twist

Fill a cocktail glass with ice and water to chill. Fill the tin side of a Boston shaker with ice. Add the brandy, Yellow Chartreuse, lemon juice, simple syrup, and Angostura bitters into the glass side of the shaker. Pour the liquid into the tin and attach the two sides. Shake until the sound of the ice changes and the combination is cold. Discard the ice and water in the cocktail glass. Strain the cocktail into the cocktail glass and garnish with the lemon twist. Serve.

Francis "Frank" Sinatra was a singer and an actor who won Academy Awards, nine Grammy Awards, Golden Globe Awards, and a Presidential Medal of Freedom. While many people don't consider Sinatra a rock star per se, he was in his time a rock star. He was known for many songs. One of them was a hit in 1961, "American Beauty Rose."

AMERICAN ROSE

1 ounce brandy
1 dash absinthe
1 dash grenadine
2 ounces peach flesh, freshly pureed
3 ounces sparkling wine

Fill a champagne flute glass with ice and water to chill. Fill the tin side of a Boston shaker with ice. Add the brandy, absinthe, grenadine, and peach puree into the glass side of the shaker. Pour the liquid into the tin and attach the two sides. Shake until the sound of the ice changes and the combination is cold. Discard the ice and water in the champagne flute. Strain the cocktail into the champagne flute and top with sparkling wine. Serve.

William "Billy" Joel is the Piano Man. With thirteen albums, Joel is also a rock star. His album *52nd Street* received two Grammy Awards, including Album of the Year. Joel has received no fewer than seven honorary doctoral degrees. His success has allowed him to afford almost any house in New York, including one on Fifth Avenue. Billy Joel received five Grammy Awards and was inducted into the Rock and Roll Hall of Fame in 1999.

*F*IFTH AVENUE

1 ounce brown crème de cacao
1 ounce apricot brandy
1 ounce cream

Add brown crème de cacao to an old-fashioned glass. Use the back of a barspoon to help layer the apricot brandy and then the cream to the glass. Serve.

Brian Warner (aka Marilyn Manson) has platinum and gold records on the wall. He is an actor and singer who has been nominated for four Grammy Awards. "The Death Song" is on the *Holy Wood* album, which was released in late 2000. Perhaps before death, one might consider a Corpse Reviver.

*C*ORPSE REVIVER

2 ounces brandy
1 ounce Calvados
1 ounce sweet vermouth
Cocktail cherry

Fill a cocktail glass with ice and water to chill. Fill a mixing glass with ice. Add the brandy, Calvados, and vermouth into the ice-filled mixing glass. With a barspoon, stir the mixture forty times. Discard the ice and water in the cocktail glass. Strain the cocktail into the cocktail glass and garnish with a cocktail cherry. Serve.

Bruce "the Boss" Springsteen is known for his many songs. "Blinded by the Light" appeared on his debut album in 1973 but was not a hit for Springsteen. Three years later, it did hit for Manfred Mann's Earth Band. The Boss would go on to have many commercial successes, including eighteen studio albums, an Academy Award, twenty Grammy Awards (and fifty nominations), a couple of Golden Globe Awards, and a Tony Award. The E Street Band has been at Springsteen's side the entire trip. Bruce Springsteen was inducted into the Rock and Roll Hall of Fame in 1999 along with his wife, Patti Scialfa, who is a member of the E Street Band.

S IDECAR

1 ½ ounces Cognac
½ ounce Cointreau
½ ounce lemon juice
Baker's sugar

Fill a cocktail glass with ice and water to chill. Fill the tin side of a Boston shaker with ice. Add the Cognac, Cointreau, and lemon juice into the glass side of the shaker. Pour the liquid into the tin and attach the two sides. Shake until the sound of the ice changes and the combination is cold. Discard the ice and water in the cocktail glass. Dip the cocktail into baker's sugar to add a sugar rim to the glass. Strain the cocktail into the cocktail glass. Serve.

Boston is a metro city from which the rock group Boston took their name. With seven albums over four decades, this band has produced classic music, including "More Than a Feeling,"

"Foreplay/Long Time," "Smokin," and "Rock and Roll Band." Each song has masterful guitar riffs, powerful percussion, and classic vocals. Boston has *not* been inducted in the Rock and Roll Hall of Fame . . . hopefully soon!

METROPOLITAN

2 ounces brandy
1 ounce sweet vermouth
½ ounce simple syrup
2 dashes Angostura bitters
Cocktail cherry

Fill a cocktail glass with ice and water to chill. Fill the tin side of a Boston shaker with ice. Add the brandy, vermouth, simple syrup, and bitters into the glass side of the shaker. Pour the liquid into the tin and attach the two sides. Shake until the sound of the ice changes and the combination is cold. Discard the ice and water in the cocktail glass. Strain the cocktail into the cocktail glass and garnish with the cocktail cherry. Serve.

In 1975, when the Sex Pistols formed, the punk band included John Lydon (aka Johnny Rotten) as the lead singer, Steve Jones on guitar, Paul Cook on drums, and Glen Matlock on bass. Matlock was replaced by John Ritchie (aka Sid Vicious). The Sex Pistols were inducted into the Rock and Roll Hall of Fame in 2006, but did not attend the induction.

Sex on the Table

1 ounce Cognac
½ ounce kirsch
½ ounce banana liqueur
1 ounce pineapple juice
1 dash orange bitters

Fill a cocktail glass with ice and water to chill. Fill the tin side of a Boston shaker with ice. Add the brandy, kirsch, banana liqueur, pineapple juice, and orange bitters into the glass side of the shaker. Pour the liquid into the tin and attach the two sides. Shake until the sound of the ice changes and the combination is cold. Discard the ice and water in the cocktail glass. Strain the cocktail into the cocktail glass. Serve.

Usher Raymond IV (aka Usher) has built an incredible R&B house for himself. He has been nominated for twenty-two Grammy Awards. He has taken eight home, including a Grammy for Best Rap/Sung Collaboration for "Yeah!" (2005) with Lil Jon and Ludacris and Best R&B Performance by a Duo or Group with Vocals with Alicia Keys for "My Boo" (2005).

House of Usher

1 ½ ounces Cognac
¼ ounce Cointreau
¼ ounce pineapple juice

¼ ounce maraschino liqueur
Orange twist

Fill a cocktail glass with ice and water to chill. Fill the tin side of a Boston shaker with ice. Add the brandy, Cointreau, pineapple juice, and maraschino liqueur into the glass side of the shaker. Pour the liquid into the tin and attach the two sides. Shake until the sound of the ice changes and the combination is cold. Discard the ice and water in the cocktail glass. Strain the cocktail into the cocktail glass and garnish with the orange twist. Serve.

Peter Gabriel was the original lead singer for Genesis before he left the group for a solo career. Gabriel is known for his hits "Big Time" and "Sledgehammer." He has six Grammy Awards. Gabriel was inducted into the Rock and Roll Hall of Fame in 2010 as a member of Genesis and in 2014 as a solo artist.

IG TIME

1 ounce Cognac
1 ounce absinthe

Prepare a shot glass. Fill the tin side of a Boston shaker with ice. Add the Cognac and absinthe into the glass side of the shaker. Pour the liquid into the tin and attach the two sides. Shake until the sound of the ice changes and the combination is cold. Strain the cocktail into the shot glass. Serve.

Alabama had thirteen nominations (seven straight) for the Best Country Performance by a Duo or Group with Vocals at the Grammy Awards in nineteen years and back-to-back wins in 1983 and 1984 to solidify their rock star status. With songs like "The Closer You Get," "Mountain Music," "She and I," and a remake of NSYNC's "God Must Have Spent a Little More Time on You," the group originally comprised of cousins has a permanent place in music history.

*A*LABAMA

1 ounce brandy
1 ounce Cointreau
½ ounce simple syrup
½ ounce lime juice
Lime twist

Fill a cocktail glass with ice and water to chill. Fill the tin side of a Boston shaker with ice. Add the brandy, Cointreau, lime juice, and simple syrup into the glass side of the shaker. Pour the liquid into the tin and attach the two sides. Shake until the sound of the ice changes and the combination is cold. Discard the ice and water in the cocktail glass. Strain the cocktail into the cocktail glass and garnish with the lime twist. Serve.

One of the classic rock 'n' roll bands is the Grateful Dead. With twenty-two albums over three decades and an army of groupies called "Dead Heads" who would travel from concert to concert, the Grateful Dead has left their mark on the rock 'n' roll landscape. The Grateful Dead was inducted into the Rock and Roll Hall of Fame in 1994.

*C*LASSIC COCKTAIL

2 ounces brandy
½ ounce Cointreau
½ ounce maraschino liqueur
Orange twist

Fill a cocktail glass with ice and water to chill. Fill the tin side of a Boston shaker with ice. Add the brandy, Cointreau, and maraschino liqueur into the glass side of the shaker. Pour the liquid into the tin and attach the two sides. Shake until the sound of the ice changes and the combination is cold. Discard the ice and water in the cocktail glass. Strain the cocktail into the cocktail glass and garnish with the orange twist. Serve.

Brandy Norwood (aka Brandy) is an R&B rock star. Nominated for Grammy Awards eleven times for songs that include "Baby," "The Boy is Mine" (she won 1999), and "Almost Doesn't Count," Brandy has released six albums. On a side note, she comes from musically talented family that includes first cousin Snoop Dogg.

*F*ANCY BRANDY

2 ounces brandy
½ ounce Cointreau
½ ounce simple syrup
1 dash Angostura bitters
Lemon twist

Fill a cocktail glass with ice and water to chill. Fill the tin side of a Boston shaker with ice. Add the brandy, Cointreau, simple syrup, and Angostura bitters into the glass side of the shaker. Pour the liquid into the tin and attach the two sides. Shake until the sound of the ice changes and the combination is cold. Discard the ice and water in the cocktail glass. Strain the cocktail into the cocktail glass and garnish with the lemon twist. Serve.

Gloria Estefan is a Cuban-American rock star. She has won three Grammy Awards and four Latin Grammy Awards. Over four decades, she has released twenty-three albums—some solo and some with her group Miami Sound Machine.

GLORIA

1 ounce brandy
½ ounce Campari
½ ounce Scotch
¼ ounce amaretto
¼ ounce dry vermouth
Orange twist

Fill a cocktail glass with ice and water to chill. Fill the tin side of a Boston shaker with ice. Add the brandy, Campari, Scotch, amaretto, and dry vermouth into the glass side of the shaker. Pour the liquid into the tin and attach the two sides. Shake until the sound of the ice changes and the combination is cold. Discard the ice and water in the cocktail glass. Strain the cocktail into the cocktail glass and garnish with the orange twist. Serve.

Shawn Carter (aka Jay-Z) has twenty-two Grammy Awards from seventy-seven nominations—more than any other rapper. He is the epitome of a rock star. "Hard Knock Life," "Crazy in Love" (with wife Beyoncé), "99 Problems," "Empire State of Mind" (with Alicia Keys), "On to the Next One" (with Swizz Beatz), and "Everything Is Love" (with Beyoncé) are just a few of his hits. Jay-Z's influence is felt internationally. He owns Armand de Brignac, which he refers to as Ace of Spades. He purchased the champagne company after a dis-agreement with the owners of Cristal, the premier brand of Louis Roederer. In his video "Show Me What You Got," Jay-Z is seen brushing off a bottle of Cristal in favor of a bottle of Ace of Spades. In 2008, when then United States Senator Barack Obama was running for president, he made a gesture of brushing his shoulders off in relation to the mudslinging that was happening on the campaign trail. Obama was referencing Jay-Z's 2004 release "Dirt Off Your Shoulder."

International Cocktail

1 ½ ounces Cognac
1 ounce triple sec
1 ounce anisette
½ ounce Vodka

Add ice and water to a cocktail glass to chill the glass. Add ice to the tin side of a Boston shaker. In the mixing glass, add vodka, anisette, triple sec, and Cognac. Pour the contents of the mixing glass into the iced tin and secure the glass to the tin. Shake the contents until the ice sounds different and the contents are cold. Open the Boston shaker. Empty the cocktail glass, and then strain the contents of the shaker into the empty glass. Serve.

William Rose Jr. (aka Axl Rose) was the lead singer for Guns N' Roses. He is currently the lead singer for AC/DC. The Indiana native is known as the voice behind such hits as "Paradise City" and "Sweet Child of Mine." Guns N' Roses was inducted into the Rock and Roll Hall of Fame in 2012—even though Rose asked not to be inducted.

$\mathcal{J}$ACK ROSE

2 ounces apple brandy
½ ounce fresh lemon juice
¼ ounce grenadine
Superfine sugar

Set up the cocktail glasses ahead of time. Dip the edge of the cocktail glass in water then dip in a plate of superfine sugar for a thin, even frost on the edge of the glass. Then freeze the glassware. Add ice to the tin side of a Boston shaker. In the mixing glass, add the apple brandy, lemon juice, and grenadine. Pour the contents of the mixing glass into the iced tin and secure the glass to the tin. Shake the contents until the ice sounds different and the contents are cold. Open the Boston shaker. Strain the contents of the shaker into the empty glass. Serve.

During the British Invasion of the United States in the mid-1960s, if the Beatles were the good boys of rock 'n' roll, the Rolling Stones were the bad boys. As things played out, the good died young, and the Stones have all survived into their late 70s and early 80s. The group has been rocking for almost six decades. Lead singer Mick Jagger is backed by Keith Richards on guitar, William Perks Jr. (aka Bill Wyman) on bass, and Charlie Watts on drums. The group has produced twenty-five albums. One of their hits was "Jumpin' Jack Flash." The Rolling Stones received three Grammy Awards and were inducted in the Rock and Roll Hall of Fame in 1989.

Jumpin' Jack Flash

1 ounce brandy
1 ounce blackberry liqueur
1 ounce orange juice
¼ ounce simple syrup

Add ice and water to an old-fashioned glass to chill the glass. Add ice to the tin side of a Boston shaker. In the mixing glass, add the simple syrup, orange juice, blackberry liqueur, and brandy. Pour the contents of the mixing glass into the iced tin and secure the glass to the tin. Shake the contents until the ice sounds different and the contents are cold. Open the Boston shaker. Strain the contents of the shaker into the ice-filled old-fashioned glass. Serve.

Vincent Eugene Craddock (aka Gene Vincent) was one of the pioneers of rock 'n' roll. He is best known for his hit "Be-Bop-A-Lula." Vincent was inducted into the Rock and Roll Hall of Fame in 1998.

Be-Bop-A-Lula

¾ ounce brandy
¾ ounce vanilla liqueur
¾ ounce cream
¾ ounce pineapple juice
¼ ounce chocolate mint liqueur

Fill a cocktail glass with ice and water to chill. Fill the tin side of a Boston shaker with ice. Add the brandy, vanilla liqueur, cream, pineapple juice, and chocolate mint liqueur into the glass side of the shaker. Pour the liquid into the tin and attach the two sides. Shake until the sound of the ice changes and the combination is cold. Discard the ice and water in the cocktail glass. Strain the cocktail. Serve.

With thirteen albums, the Norwegian Band TNT are rockers who have enjoyed the ride for almost four decades.

TNT

2 ounces brandy
1 ounce triple sec
¼ ounce pastis

Add ice and water to a cocktail glass to chill the glass. Add ice to the tin side of a Boston shaker. In the mixing glass, add the brandy, triple sec, and pastis. Pour the contents of the mixing glass into the iced tin and secure the glass to the tin. Shake the contents until the ice sounds different and the contents are cold. Open the Boston shaker. Empty the cocktail glass, and then strain the contents of the shaker into the empty glass. Serve.

Whiskey (whisky) is the largest differentiated spirit category. This spirit is traditionally made in Scotland, Ireland, Canada, and the United States. Whiskey is distilled from beer made from grain. Each tradition uses different grain or a grain mixture for the distiller's beer. The beer is then distilled into a clear spirit and aged in oak barrels for a short or extended period. The longer the whiskey is aged, the higher the price of the spirit. Most Scotch whisky is made from malt and grain whiskies and is aged in a variety of used barrels, including bourbon, sherry, and porto barrels. Scotch has a unique smoked, peaty flavor and aroma. Most Scotch is aged for at least four years but can be aged for much, much longer. Irish whiskey has a light and mild flavor and aroma and can be made from a variety of grains. This spirit is aged for at least three years, but much is aged longer. Canadian whisky is mild flavored, made from multiple grains, and aged for at least three years. Bourbon is one of the most highly regulated whiskies that is made in the United States (although 95 percent is made in Kentucky). It is made from 51 percent corn (most bourbon distillers use more—closer to 65–75 percent). As bourbon comes off the still, it must be less than 160 proof. Only water can be added to bourbon. As bourbon is added to newly charred oak barrels, the proof can't exceed 125 proof and can't be less than 80 proof. There is no minimum age for bourbon, but if the bourbon is aged less than two years, there must be an age statement on the label. Most bourbon is aged for at least four years. Other whiskies are usually defined by the grain from which they are primary made. For example, corn whiskey is at least 80 percent corn, rye whiskey is at least 51 percent rye, and wheat whiskey is at least 51 percent wheat.

WHISKEY COCKTAILS

The Manhattans are an R&B group from New Jersey who are known from the songs "Kiss and Say Goodbye," "Forever by

Your Side," and "Shining Star." They formed in 1962 and are still active today. The Manhattans received a Grammy Award in 1980 for Best R&B Performance by a Duo or Group with Vocals for "Shining Star."

*M*ANHATTAN

2 ounces rye or bourbon
1 ounce sweet vermouth
1 or 2 dashes Angostura bitters
Cocktail cherry

Fill a cocktail glass with ice and water to chill. Fill a mixing glass with ice. Add the whiskey, vermouth, and Angostura bitters into the mixing glass. With a mixing spoon, stir forty times or until the mixture is cold. Discard the ice and water in the cocktail glass. Strain the cocktail into the cocktail glass and garnish with the cocktail cherry. Serve.

LeAnn Rimes has produced seventeen albums in twenty-eight years and has claimed two Grammy Awards, including Best New Artist (1997). Early in her career, she was tapped to sing four songs for the soundtrack of the movie *Coyote Ugly* and appear as herself in the movie. The mark of a true rock star!

*C*OYOTE GIRL

1 ½ ounces bourbon
1 ounce Southern Comfort
1 ounce lemon juice

Fill a cocktail glass with ice and water to chill. Fill the tin side of a Boston shaker with ice. Add the bourbon, Southern Comfort, and lemon juice into the glass side of the shaker. Pour the liquid into the tin and attach the two sides. Shake until the sound of the ice changes and the combination is cold. Discard the ice and water in the cocktail glass. Strain the cocktail into the cocktail glass. Serve.

The trio Rush formed in 1968 in Toronto, Canada. In fifty years, the group has produced twenty-four gold, fourteen platinum, and three multiplatinum albums. Geddy Lee Weinrib (aka Geddy Lee) is the lead singer and is backed by Alexandar Zivojinovich (aka Alex Lifeson) on guitar and Neil Peart on drums. They have produced nineteen albums. Rush was inducted into the Rock and Roll Hall of Fame in 2013.

CANADA

1 ½ ounces Canadian whisky
¾ ounce Cointreau
¾ ounce maple syrup

Fill a cocktail glass with ice and water to chill. Fill the tin side of a Boston shaker with ice. Add the Canadian whisky, Cointreau, and maple syrup into the glass side of the shaker. Pour the liquid into the tin and attach the two sides. Shake until the sound of the ice changes and the combination is cold. Discard the ice and water in the cocktail glass. Strain the cocktail into the cocktail glass. Serve.

Kim Wilson is the one constant over the past four decades with the Texas rock group the Fabulous Thunderbirds. Wilson also penned two hits the group enjoyed in the 1980s, "Tuff Enuff" and "Wrap It Up." The group enjoyed the guitar stylings of Jimmie Vaughan, the older brother of blues legend Stevie Ray Vaughan.

T-Bird

1 ounce Canadian whisky
¾ ounce amaretto
2 ounces pineapple juice
1 ounce orange juice
¼ ounce grenadine
Orange slice

Fill a highball glass with ice. Fill the tin side of a Boston shaker with ice. Add the Canadian whisky, amaretto, pineapple juice, orange juice, and grenadine into the glass side of the shaker. Pour the liquid into the tin and attach the two sides. Shake until the sound of the ice changes and the combination is cold. Strain the cocktail into the ice-filled highball glass and garnish with the orange slice. Serve.

With nine studio albums over three decades and record-breaking sales, the Backstreet Boys have made their mark on the music world. The five vocalists include Kevin Richardson, Brian Littrell, Nick Carter, Howie Dorough, and A. J. McLean. The group was formed in Orlando, Florida.

*B*ACK STREET ROMEO

1 ounce whiskey
½ ounce Irish cream liqueur

Prepare a shot glass. Fill the tin side of a Boston shaker with ice. Add the whiskey and Irish cream liqueur into the glass side of the shaker. Pour the liquid into the tin and attach the two sides. Shake until the sound of the ice changes and the combination is cold. Strain the cocktail into the shot glass. Serve.

Sid Vicious was only twenty-one years old when he passed away of a drug overdose. At the time, he was under suspicion of murdering his twenty-year-old girlfriend, Nancy Spungen. Actor Gary Oldman portrayed Vicious in the movie *Sid and Nancy*. Nancy was portrayed by Chloe Webb. Vicious was inducted into the Rock and Roll Hall of Fame in 2006 as a member of the Sex Pistols.

*S*ID VICIOUS

1 ounce whiskey
1 ounce gin
½ ounce sweet vermouth
1 dash Angostura bitters
1 dash Worcestershire sauce

Fill an old-fashioned glass with ice. Add the Worcestershire sauce, Angostura bitters, whiskey, gin, and vermouth and stir. Serve.

Thomas DeCarlo Callaway (aka CeeLo Green) has five Grammy Awards to his credit. His collaboration with songwriter and fellow rock star Bruno Mars, Ari Levine, and Phillip Lawrence paid dividends for the single "Fuck You!" The single won the Grammy for Best Urban/Alternative Performance at the Fifty-Third Grammy Awards in 2010.

UCK YOU

½ ounce Jack Daniel's Tennessee whiskey
½ ounce bourbon
½ ounce tequila
½ ounce rum
½ ounce Goldschläger
½ ounce blueberry liqueur

Fill a highball glass with ice. Fill the tin side of a Boston shaker with ice. Add the Jack Daniel's, bourbon, tequila, rum, Goldschläger, and blueberry liqueur into the glass side of the shaker. Pour the liquid into the tin and attach the two sides. Shake until the sound of the ice changes and the combination is cold. Strain the cocktail into the ice-filled highball glass. Serve.

Ohio rock band Red Sun Rising has released four albums—two independent and two studio. Their album *Thread* was released in March 2018 and included the first single to be released off the album, "Deathwish," which was released in January. This Deathwish cocktail includes bourbon, Jägermeister, and Rumple Minze.

EATH WISH

½ ounce bourbon
½ ounce Rumple Minze
½ ounce Jägermeister

Prepare a shot glass. Fill the tin side of a Boston shaker with ice. Add the bourbon, Rumple Minze, and Jägermeister into the glass side of the shaker. Pour the liquid into the tin and attach the two sides. Shake until the sound of the ice changes and the combination is cold. Strain the cocktail into the shot glass. Serve.

Nick Perri is a guitarist and songwriter from Pennsylvania who has been a member of several bands, including Silvertide. According to the band's website, they toured with Van Halen, Mötley Crüe, Foo Fighters, ZZ Top, Puddle of Mud, Maroon 5, Kid Rock, and Aerosmith, to name a few, before breaking up. They would eventually get back together, but in the meantime, Perri joined a band called the Darling Stilettos for a short period of time.

STILETTO

1 ½ ounces whiskey
1 ½ ounces amaretto
½ ounce lemon juice
Lemon twist

Fill an old-fashioned glass with ice. Fill the tin side of a Boston shaker with ice. Add the whiskey, amaretto, and lemon juice into the glass side of the shaker. Pour the liquid into the tin and attach the two sides. Shake until the sound of the ice changes and the combination is cold. Strain the cocktail into the old-fashioned glass and garnish with the lemon twist. Serve.

Three Dog Night sang "An Old Fashioned Love Song" on their *Harmony* album, but Paul Williams wrote the hit. Williams wrote many hits for many artists, including "Evergreen" for the Barbara Streisand version of *A Star Is Born*. For his efforts, Williams won a Grammy and an Oscar.

OLD-FASHIONED

2 ounces whiskey
2 dashes Angostura bitters
1 sugar cube
½ ounce warm water
Cocktail cherry
Orange twist

Prepare an old-fashioned glass. Add the sugar cube, water, and Angostura bitters to the old-fashioned glass. Muddle the sugar into the water and bitters. Once combined, add the whiskey and then some ice. Stir and add more ice. Stir again. Garnish with a twist and cocktail cherry. Serve.

With fourteen studio albums between the mid-1970s and the mid-1990s, the punk rock group Ramones looked like a happy family on the surface. In reality, none of the band members were related, but they all adopted the last name Ramone; the original four included Jeffrey Hyman (aka Joey Ramone), Douglas Colvin (aka Dee Dee Ramone), John Cummings (aka Johnny Ramone), and Thomas Erdelyi (aka Tommy Ramone). Replacement members included Marc Bell (aka Marky Ramone), Christopher Joseph Ward (aka C. J. Ramone), Richard Reinhardt (aka Richie Ramone), and Clem Burke (aka Elvis Ramone) Their 1976 self-titled album included the single, "53rd & 3rd," cross streets in New York City. The Ramones were inducted into the Rock and Roll Hall of Fame in 2002 and received the Grammy Lifetime Achievement Award in 2011. By 2014, all of the original lineup had passed away.

*N*EW YORK COCKTAIL

1 ½ ounces whiskey
½ ounce lemon juice
¼ ounce simple syrup
Splash grenadine
Lemon twist

Fill a cocktail glass with ice and water to chill. Fill the tin side of a Boston shaker with ice. Add the whiskey, lemon juice, simple syrup, and grenadine into the glass side of the shaker. Pour the liquid into the tin and attach the two sides. Shake until the sound of the ice changes and the combination is cold. Discard the ice and water in the cocktail glass. Strain the cocktail into the cocktail glass and garnish with the lemon twist. Serve.

Chris Stapleton is a rock star country artist. The Kentucky native has received five Grammy Awards on three studio albums between 2015 and 2017. The first single from *From a Room: Volume 2* is "Millionaire," a song about the value of love.

*M*ILLIONAIRE COCKTAIL

1 ½ ounces whiskey
½ ounce Cointreau
1 ounce egg white
¼ ounce grenadine
Orange twist

Fill a cocktail glass with ice and water to chill. Fill the tin side of a Boston shaker with ice. Add the whiskey, Cointreau, egg white, and grenadine into the glass side of the shaker. Pour the liquid into the tin and attach the two sides. Shake until the sound of the ice changes and the combination is cold. Discard the ice and water in the cocktail glass. Strain the cocktail into the cocktail glass and garnish with the orange twist. Serve.

Christopher Wallace (aka the Notorious B.I.G., Biggy Smalls, or just Biggy) was born in Brooklyn. Biggy had a short career, dying in a drive-by shooting at the age of twenty-four in 1997. His murder has never been solved. However, in many ways his success transcended death. He only had two albums cut before he died, but four have been added since, including *Life After Death*, which was released about two weeks after the shooting.

*B*ROOKLYN

2 ounces rye or bourbon
1 ounce dry vermouth
¼ ounce maraschino liqueur
2 dashes Angostura bitters
Cocktail cherry

Fill a cocktail glass with ice and water to chill. Fill a mixing glass with ice. Add the whiskey, vermouth, maraschino liqueur, and Angostura bitters into the glass. Mix the combination with a barspoon at least forty times. Discard the ice and water in the cocktail glass. Strain the cocktail into the cocktail glass and garnish with the cocktail cherry. Serve.

Over fifty years, the Commodores have had fourteen studio albums and a Grammy Award for their hit "Nightshift." Other Commodores' hits include, "Easy," "Three Times a Lady," "Brick House," and "Lady (You Bring Me Up)." The only original member is William "Wak" King, and he is joined by Walter Orange and J. D. Nicholas.

$\mathcal{C}$OMMODORE

1 ½ ounces bourbon

1 ounce crème de cacao

1 ounce lemon juice

1 dash grenadine

Fill a cocktail glass with ice and water to chill. Fill the tin side of a Boston shaker with ice. Add the bourbon, crème de cacao, lemon juice, and grenadine into the glass side of the shaker. Pour the liquid into the tin and attach the two sides. Shake until the sound of the ice changes and the combination is cold. Discard the ice and water in the cocktail glass. Strain the cocktail into the cocktail glass. Serve.

Robert Ritchie (aka Kid Rock) is a singer/songwriter who has eleven studio albums and a career that spans three decades. Kid Rock cites his success by singing, "I've been on the cover of the Rolling Stone," in his single "You Never Met a Motherfucker Quite Like Me" off of his fifth album, *Cocky*. His success has spanned rap, rock, and country music genres. The single "Cowboy" was featured on his fourth album, *Devil without a Cause*. Kid Rock is a fan of whiskey and reviewed *Beam, Straight Up: The Bold Story of the First Family of Bourbon* by Fred Noe, the master distiller for Jim Beam.

*C*owboy Cocktail

2 ounces whiskey
½ ounce cream

Fill a cocktail glass with ice and water to chill. Fill the tin side of a Boston shaker with ice. Add the whiskey and cream into the glass side of the shaker. Pour the liquid into the tin and attach the two sides. Shake until the sound of the ice changes and the combination is cold. Discard the ice and water in the cocktail glass. Strain the cocktail into the cocktail glass. Serve.

The Irish Group U2 sounds like a duo, but the four members include front man Paul Hewson (aka Bono Vox or Bono), David Evans (aka the Edge) on guitar, Adam Clayton on bass, and Larry Mullen Jr. on drums. The Dublin-based group have fourteen studio albums and twenty-two Grammy Awards; it is an amazing feat, as their first Grammy did not come until their fifth album, *The Joshua Tree*. U2 was inducted into the Rock and Roll Hall of Fame in 2005.

*D*ublin Doubler

1 ounce Irish whiskey
1 ounce Irish cream liqueur

Prepare a shot glass. Fill the tin side of a Boston shaker with ice. Add the Irish whiskey and the Irish cream liqueur into the glass side of the shaker. Pour the liquid into the tin and attach the two sides. Shake until the sound of the ice changes and the combination is cold. Strain the cocktail into the shot glass. Serve.

Marshall Mathers III (aka Eminem or Slim Shady) released ten studio albums between 1996 and 2018. In his song "The Real Slim Shady," he raps, "You think I give a damn about a Grammy? Half of you critics can't even stomach me, let alone stand me." Eminem has received fifteen Grammy Awards. He also won a Best Original Song Oscar in 2003 for "Lose Yourself."

LONE MARSHALL

1 ounce bourbon
1 ounce peach schnapps
½ ounce Southern Comfort
½ ounce sour mix
2 ounces orange juice
Orange slice

Fill a highball glass with ice. Fill the tin side of a Boston shaker with ice. Add the bourbon, peach schnapps, Southern Comfort, sour mix, and orange juice into the glass side of the shaker. Pour the liquid into the tin and attach the two sides. Shake until the sound of the ice changes and the combination is cold. Strain the cocktail into the ice-filled highball glass and garnish with the orange slice. Serve.

Ralph Flanagan's music was pre–rock 'n' roll, although he lived long enough to see modern rock 'n' roll. The Ohio native's music was more akin to big band, but during his career, he cut ten studio albums. In the 1950s, one of his hits was "Hot Toddy."

WHISKEY TODDY

1 cube of sugar
2 ounces hot water
2 ounces whiskey

Add the sugar cube and hot water to a coffee mug. Allow the sugar to melt into the water, and then add the whiskey. Serve.

Harry Connick Jr. is a singer-actor who is also a rock star with twenty-six studio albums. The New Orleans native has received three Grammy Awards and two Emmys. His breakthrough was in 1989 with the *When Harry Met Sally* soundtrack. His smooth voice and youthful look helped catapult him into stardom. His first Grammy Award was for Best Jazz Male Vocal Performance for the movie's soundtrack. This recipe is my adaptation of the cocktail recipe for a Rock Star at the Café Adelaide in New Orleans in the book *In the Land of Cocktails: Recipes and Adventures from the Cocktail Chicks*, by Ti Adelaide Martin and Lally Brennan.

OCK STAR

2 ounces bourbon
2 ounces citrus-flavored energy drink
1 splash cola

Fill an old-fashioned glass with ice. Add the bourbon and energy drink, stir, and then top with cola. Serve.

With eighteen studio albums and four Grammy Awards, Aaron Neville is a rock star R&B and soul singer, although there was a twenty-year gap between his first and second albums. He also cut albums with his three brothers as the Neville Brothers. His song "Tell It Like It Is" a classic and was featured in the soundtrack for *The Big Easy*. His duo with Linda Ronstadt, "Don't Know Much," is a great example of his work. The two shared the 1990 Grammy Award for Best Pop Performance by a Duo or Group with Vocals. In 2008, the Sazerac became the official cocktail of New Orleans.

$\int$AZERAC

¼ ounce absinthe
1 sugar cube
3 dashes Peychaud's bitters
2 ounces whiskey
Orange twist
Lemon twist

Add the absinthe to an old-fashioned glass. Swirl the glass and pour out the absinthe. Add the sugar cube to the bottom of the glass and top with Peychaud's bitters. Add the whiskey and stir. Fill the glass with ice. Garnish with the orange twist and lemon twist. Serve.

Modern alcoholic concoctions are made from an endless combination of alcoholic beverages from many categories, including beer, wine, spirits, and liqueurs. Beer and wine are both fermented beverages. Beer is made by boiling grains to extract the sugars for fermenting to an average of 5 percent alcohol by volume. Wine is usually made from grapes. The grapes are pressed to extract the juice, which is then fermented. Wine varies in alcohol volume from 5 percent to 15 percent, with fortified wine being even higher. Fortified wine is wine with added brandy. Liqueurs are flavored and sweetened alcoholic beverage that are featured in many cocktails and serve as standalone after-dinner drinks also known as cordials. The alcohol by volume range for most liqueurs is from 17 percent (34 proof) to 30 percent (60 proof) but can be higher than 50 percent (100 proof).

OTHER COCKTAILS

The next five cocktails come from the mind of my mixology mentor Gary Gruver, who is now the Senior Beverage Manager for Global Operations at Marriot International. Gary has encouraged me over the years and has always been available for advice. Gary facilitated my first bartending gig at the one-night pre–Kentucky Derby party, Unbridled Eve at the Galt House in Louisville, Kentucky. I bartended that party three years in a row! Another event that Gary called on me to help bartend was for a VIP backstage bar at the 2015 Louder Than Life Festival hosted by Jägermeister. The October outdoor event featured ZZ Top, Lynyrd Skynyrd, Seether, 3 Doors Down, and many others. The weather that weekend was cold and rainy. I remember little feeling in my fingers as I prepared drinks. Gary and I served five different drinks to the bands and other people who had backstage passes. He was kind enough to share the recipes. These are drinks that were consumed by rock stars!

Kentucky Jäger Sour

1 ounce Larceny Bourbon
1 ounce Jägermeister
¾ ounce fresh lemon juice
½ ounce simple syrup
½ ounce egg white
Lemon wheel or wedge
Cocktail cherry

Fill an old-fashioned glass with ice. Fill the tin side of a Boston shaker with ice. Add the bourbon, Jägermeister, lemon juice, simple syrup, and egg white into the glass side of the shaker. Pour the liquid into the tin and attach the two sides. Shake until the sound of the ice changes and the combination is cold. Strain the cocktail into the ice-filled old-fashioned glass and garnish with the lemon and cocktail cherry. Serve.

GERMAN COKE FLOAT

1 1/2 ounces Jägermeister
1 ounce condensed milk
4 ounces Mexican Coke

Fill an old-fashioned glass with ice. Fill the tin side of a Boston shaker with ice. Add the Jägermeister and condensed milk into the glass side of the shaker. Pour the liquid into the tin and attach the two sides. Shake until the sound of the ice changes and the combination is cold. Strain the cocktail into the ice-filled old-fashioned glass and pour Coke over the mixture. Serve.

This drink was originally made with Jägermeister Spice, which is no longer available. The drink called for 1 ounce Jägermeister and ½ ounce Jägermeister Spice. I have combined the two for this cocktail.

JÄGER TIKI

½ ounce Ron Zacapa Rum
1 ½ ounces Jägermeister
3 ounces pineapple juice
3 dashes Angostura bitters
torched cinnamon
Fresh sage for garnish

Fill an old-fashioned glass with ice. Fill the tin side of a Boston shaker with ice. Add the rum, Jägermeister, pineapple, and Angostura bitters into the glass side of the shaker. Pour the liquid into the tin and attach the two sides. Shake until the sound of the ice changes and the combination is cold. Strain the cocktail into the old-fashioned glass. Light a small torch above the drink and sprinkle the cinnamon through the flame. Slap the fresh sage on the back of your hand, and then garnish the drink with the sprig. Serve.

This cocktail originally featured equal parts Jägermeister and Jägermeister Spice. I have combined the two in this recipe.

Louder Than Hot Chocolate

¾ ounce RumChata
1 ½ ounces Jägermeister
3 ounces hot chocolate
2 dashes Angostura bitters
Toasted marshmallows

Prepare an Irish coffee glass or coffee mug with hot water. Once the mug is warm, discard the water. Add the RumChata, Jägermeister, and prepared hot chocolate. Top with the Angostura bitters. Then add marshmallows. Toast with a small torch. Serve.

SPICED MULE

¾ ounce Sombra Mezcal
1 ounce Jägermeister
½ lime
4 ounces Gosling's Ginger Beer

*Fill an old-fashioned glass with ice. Fill the tin side
of a Boston shaker with ice. Add the Sombra Mezcal,
Jägermeister, and juice from the ½ lime (retain the lime for
garnish) into the glass side of the shaker. Pour the liquid into
the tin and attach the two sides. Shake until the sound of the
ice changes and the combination is cold. Strain the cocktail
into the ice-filled old-fashioned glass. Top with the ginger
beer and garnish with the lime. Serve.*

"Alright, new drink. One part Alizé, one part Cristal—Thug
Passion." Tupac Shakur (aka 2Pac—he was born Lesane
Crooks) starts his song "Thug Passion" with a cocktail recipe.
"Thug Passion" is on the second disc of his *All Eyez on Me* album. Tupac was born in Harlem but became a huge influence
in West Coast hip hop with ten studio albums. Six albums
were released after he passed away at the age of twenty-five
from a drive-by shooting. He was nominated for six Grammy
Awards but did not receive one. Tupac Shakur was inducted
into the Rock and Roll Hall of Fame in 2017.

*T*HUG **PASSION**

3 ounces Alizé Gold Passion
3 ounces sparkling wine (Tupac calls for Cristal)

Add Alizé Gold Passion into a champagne flute and then top with sparkling wine. Serve.

Lionel Richie is a singer/songwriter who has multiple successful careers. He was a member of the Commodores and now enjoys a solo career. He is also an actor, record producer, and judge on *American Idol*. He worked on nine albums with the Commodores and has ten solo albums. He has received four Grammy Awards with thirty-two nominations, a Golden Globe, and an Academy Award. He won the Oscar for "Say You, Say Me," which was featured in the movie *White Nights*. His song "All Night Long" was nominated for four Grammys at the Twenty-Sixth Grammy Awards. The next year at the Twenty-Seventh Grammy Awards, he won for Album of the Year for *Can't Slow Down*, the album that featured "All Night Long."

*A*LL **NIGHT LONG**

½ ounce rum
½ ounce coconut rum
½ ounce coffee liqueur
½ ounce white crème de cacao
4 ounces pineapple juice

2 ounces sour mix
Pineapple wedge

Fill a hurricane glass with ice. Fill the tin side of a Boston shaker with ice. Add the rum, coconut rum, coffee liqueur, crème de cacao, pineapple juice, and sour mix into the glass side of the shaker. Pour the liquid into the tin and attach the two sides. Shake until the sound of the ice changes and the combination is cold. Strain the cocktail into the ice-filled hurricane glass and garnish with a pineapple wedge. Serve.

As if he were King Midas of Greek myth, almost everything that Justin Timberlake touches seems to turn to gold—or perhaps platinum is a better description. First, he was a member of the All-New Mickey Mouse Club and then a member of the boy band NSYNC. A solo career followed, and more recently he has been the founder of Sauza 901 Tequila. Timberlake is a master at collaboration, and there are many examples, including Jimmy Fallon, Jay-Z, Andy Samberg, Lady Gaga, and Chris Stapleton. He has received ten Grammy Awards, four Emmy Awards, and an Academy Award nomination. He helped create three albums with NSYNC and five more solo albums. His musical hits include "Can't Stop the Feeling!" "Suit and Tie," "What Goes Around . . . Comes Around," "Sexy-Back," "Drink You Away," and "TKO."

TKO

---

1 ounce Sauza 901 Tequila
1 ounce coffee liqueur
1 ounce ouzo

Fill an old-fashioned glass with ice. Fill the tin side of a Boston shaker with ice. Add the tequila, coffee liqueur, and ouzo into the glass side of the shaker. Pour the liquid into the tin and attach the two sides. Shake until the sound of the ice changes and the combination is cold. Strain the cocktail into the ice-filled old-fashioned glass. Serve.

The Police were a British trio that included Sting, Andy Summers, and Stewart Copeland (covered earlier in the book with the cocktail Bad Sting). They won six Grammy Awards and were inducted into the Rock and Roll Hall of Fame in 2003. Their first album, *Outlandos d'Amour*, contains their breakout single, "Roxanne."

OXANNE

¾ ounce vodka
¾ ounce peach schnapps
½ ounce amaretto
½ ounce orange juice
½ ounce cranberry juice cocktail
Orange twist

Fill an old-fashioned glass with ice. Fill the tin side of a Boston shaker with ice. Add the vodka, peach schnapps, amaretto, orange juice, and cranberry juice into the glass side of the shaker. Pour the liquid into the tin and attach the two sides. Shake until the sound of the ice changes and the combination is cold. Strain the cocktail into the old-fashioned glass and garnish with the orange twist. Serve.

When a group has a hit, the most difficult task for a rock band is to cover the same song paying tribute to the original and at the same time creating something different. The song "Lady Marmalade," a song about a New Orleans prostitute, was first covered in 1974 by the group Labelle, a trio that included Patti LaBelle, Nona Hendryx, and Sarah Dash, and reached number one in the United States. In 1998, All Saints covered the song for a United Kingdom number one. All Saints is a female quartet that includes Shaznay Lewis, Melanie Blatt, and sisters Nicole and Natalie Appleton. In 2001, a collaboration by Christina Aguilera, Mya, P!nk, and Lil' Kim hit number one in the United States and received the Grammy Award for Best Pop Collaboration with Vocals in 2001. The song includes the French phrase, "*Voulez-vous coucher avec moi (ce soir)*?" The English translation is "Do you want to sleep with me (tonight)?"

Moulin Rouge

2 ounces sloe gin
1 ounce sweet vermouth
1 dash Angostura bitters
Lemon twist

Fill a cocktail glass with ice and water to chill. Fill the tin side of a Boston shaker with ice. Add the sloe gin, sweet vermouth, and bitters into the glass side of the shaker. Pour the liquid into the tin and attach the two sides. Shake until the sound of the ice changes and the combination is cold. Discard the ice and water in the cocktail glass. Strain the cocktail into the cocktail glass and garnish with the lemon twist. Serve.

Joan Larkin (aka Joan Jett) has twelve studio albums. Her hits include "I Love Rock and Roll," "I Hate Myself for Loving You," "Bad Reputation," and "Crimson and Clover." Joan Jett and the Blackhearts were inducted into the Rock and Roll Hall of Fame in 2015.

OCK 'N' ROLL

1 ounce vodka
1 ounce chocolate mint liqueur

Prepare a shot glass. Fill the tin side of a Boston shaker with ice. Add the vodka and the chocolate mint liqueur into the glass side of the shaker. Pour the liquid into the tin and attach the two sides. Shake until the sound of the ice changes and the combination is cold. Strain the cocktail into the shot glass. Serve.

Elvis Presley was known as the King of Rock 'n' Roll. He recorded twenty-four studio albums and seventeen soundtrack albums and starred in more than thirty films. Presley received three Grammy Awards and the Grammy Lifetime Achievement Award. Elvis Presley was inducted into the Rock and Roll Hall of Fame in 1986. The King was known for his love of peanut butter and banana sandwiches.

LVIS PRESLEY

½ ounce vodka
½ ounce Frangelico

½ ounce crème de banana
¼ ounce Irish cream liqueur

Prepare a shot glass. Fill the tin side of a Boston shaker with ice. Add the vodka, Frangelico, crème de banana, and Irish cream liqueur into the glass side of the shaker. Pour the liquid into the tin and attach the two sides. Shake until the sound of the ice changes and the combination is cold. Strain the cocktail into the shot glass. Serve.

Pink Floyd was an English rock band known for the albums *Dark Side of the Moon* and *The Wall*. The group consisted of Nick Mason, Roger Waters, Richard Wright, Syd Barrett, and David Gilmour. The received a single Grammy Award. Pink Floyd was inducted into the Rock and Roll Hall of Fame in 1996.

INK FLOYD

½ ounce vodka
½ ounce peach schnapps
½ ounce cranberry juice cocktail
½ ounce grapefruit juice

Prepare a shot glass. Fill the tin side of a Boston shaker with ice. Add the vodka, peach schnapps, cranberry juice cocktail, and grapefruit juice into the glass side of the shaker. Pour the liquid into the tin and attach the two sides. Shake until the sound of the ice changes and the combination is cold. Strain the cocktail into the shot glass. Serve.

Prince Rogers Nelson (aka Prince and the Artist Formerly Known as Prince) was a singer/songwriter. The Minneapolis native received seven Grammy Awards, a Golden Globe, and an Academy Award. He released more than thirty-five albums. Prince was inducted into the Rock and Roll Hall of Fame in 2004. In 1985, he received his Academy Award for Best Original Song Score, as well as two of his Grammy Awards, for the movie *Purple Rain* and the song of the same name.

PURPLE RAIN

½ ounce vodka
½ ounce rum
½ ounce gin
½ ounce blue curaçao
½ ounce cranberry juice cocktail
4 ounces lemon-lime soda
Orange twist

Fill a highball glass with ice. Fill the tin side of a Boston shaker with ice. Add the vodka, rum, gin, blue curaçao, and cranberry juice cocktail into the glass side of the shaker. Pour the liquid into the tin and attach the two sides. Shake until the sound of the ice changes and the combination is cold. Strain the cocktail into the highball glass and top with lemon-lime soda. Garnish with the orange twist. Serve.

The Jackson family is a musically prolific family. The Jackson 5 was founded in the mid-1960s. The group included brothers Michael, Jermaine, Jackie, Marlon, and Tito and later included Randy. The Jackson 5 were inducted into the Rock and Roll Hall of Fame in 1997. Some of the brothers enjoyed solo careers. During his solo career, Michael received thirteen Grammy Awards and was inducted in the Rock and Roll Hall of Fame in 2001. Their sister Janet Jackson received five Grammy Awards and was inducted in the Rock and Roll Hall of Fame in 2019.

*J*ACKSON 5

⅓ ounce bourbon
⅓ ounce Tennessee whiskey
⅓ ounce rye whiskey
⅓ ounce tequila
⅓ ounce Jägermeister

Prepare a shot glass. Fill the tin side of a Boston shaker with ice. Add the bourbon, Tennessee whiskey, rye whiskey, tequila, and Jägermeister into the glass side of the shaker. Pour the liquid into the tin and attach the two sides. Shake until the sound of the ice changes and the combination is cold. Strain the cocktail into the shot glass. Serve.

Gene Simmons, the bass guitarist and lead singer for KISS, is known for his tongue.

*E*IGHT-INCH TONGUE

½ ounce vodka
½ ounce brandy

½ ounce Southern Comfort
½ ounce peach schnapps
½ ounce amaretto
4 ounces cranberry juice cocktail
Orange twist

Fill a highball glass with ice. Fill the tin side of a Boston shaker with ice. Add the vodka, brandy, Southern Comfort, peach schnapps, and amaretto into the glass side of the shaker. Pour the liquid into the tin and attach the two sides. Shake until the sound of the ice changes and the combination is cold. Strain the cocktail into the highball glass and top with cranberry juice cocktail. Stir and garnish with the orange twist. Serve.

A relatively new group is the Charm City Devils. They formed in 2007 in Baltimore. The group includes front man John Allen, Victor Karrera on guitar, Nick Kay on guitar, Anthony Arambula on bass, and Jason Heiser on drums. They have produced three studio albums.

SIMPLE CHARM

¾ ounce Cognac
¾ ounce coffee liqueur
¾ ounce amaretto
⅓ ounce cream

Fill a cocktail glass with ice and water to chill. Fill the tin side of a Boston shaker with ice. Add the Cognac, coffee liqueur, amaretto, and cream into the glass side of the shaker.

Pour the liquid into the tin and attach the two sides. Shake until the sound of the ice changes and the combination is cold. Discard the ice and water in the cocktail glass. Strain the cocktail into the cocktail glass. Serve.

The 27 Club is an exclusive group that most rock stars try to avoid. Some of the members include Jimi Hendrix, Janis Joplin, Jim Morrison, Brian Jones, Kurt Cobain, Mia Zapata, and Amy Winehouse, to name a few. This original cocktail is to honor those rockers whose time was cut short. I hope they would enjoy this cocktail.

*T*HE 27 CLUB

1 ½ ounces Green Chartreuse
4 ½ ounces sweet sparkling wine
1 dash Angostura bitters
1 dash Peychaud's bitters

Add the Green Chartreuse to a champagne flute. Pour the sparkling wine into the flute, then float the bitters on top of the drink. Serve.

New jack swing is a genre of music that included many groups in the 1980s and 1990s, including Boyz II Men, Bell Biv DeVoe, Blackstreet, En Vogue, SWV, Tony! Toni! Toné!, Keith Sweat, Janet Jackson, Paula Abdul, Baby Face, Mary J. Blige, and Bobby Brown, to name just a few of the artists. This drink honors all of them and is named for Another Bad Creation (ABC).

*A*BC

1 ounce amaretto

1 ounce Baileys Irish Cream

1 ounce Cointreau

Fill a highball glass with ice. Fill the tin side of a Boston shaker with ice. Add the amaretto, Baileys Irish Cream, and Cointreau into the glass side of the shaker. Pour the liquid into the tin and attach the two sides. Shake until the sound of the ice changes and the combination is cold. Discard the ice and water in the cocktail glass. Strain the cocktail into the cocktail glass. Serve.

One of the first songs that I remember is "Yellow Submarine." The Beatles hit with this song in 1966, and it quickly was a number one hit worldwide. It is one of the few songs with Ringo Starr on lead vocals.

*Y*ELLOW SUBMARINE

2 ounces reposado tequila

12 ounces beer

Lime wedge

Fill a shot glass with tequila. Invert a beer mug. Put the shot glass inside the mug against its bottom. Holding the shot glass, turn the mug over right-side up so that the tequila does not leak out. Carefully pour a beer into the mug. Garnish with a lime. Serve.

The 1999 collaboration between Carlos Santana and Rob Thomas was both "Smooth" and sweet! The song is called "Smooth," which won three Grammy Awards for the two artists, including Record of the Year, Song of the Year, and Best Pop Collaboration with vocals. The group Santana, led by Carlos, received eight Grammy Awards and three Latin Grammy Awards. Carlos Santana received an additional two Grammy Awards. The group Santana was inducted into the Rock and Roll Hall of Fame in 1998.

*S*MOOTH AND SWEET

½ ounce amaretto
½ ounce blackberry liqueur
¼ ounce pineapple juice

Prepare a shot glass. Fill the tin side of a Boston shaker with ice. Add the blackberry liqueur, amaretto, and pineapple juice into the glass side of the shaker. Pour the liquid into the tin and attach the two sides. Shake until the sound of the ice changes and the combination is cold. Strain the cocktail into the shot glass. Serve.

Daft Punk is a French duo that specializes in electric dance music. The duo includes Guillaume Emmanuel de Homem-Christo (aka Guy-Manuel de Homem-Christo) and Thomas Bangalter. Since 1997, they have produced four studio

albums that have produced twelve nominations for Grammy
Awards, receiving six.

*F*RENCH **125**

1 ounce brandy
1 ounce sour mix
4 ounces sparkling wine
Orange twist

*Fill a Collins glass with ice. Add the brandy and sour mix.
Top with sparkling wine, stir, and garnish with and orange
twist. Serve.*

Enrique Martin Morales (aka Ricky Martin) is a singer also
known as the King of Latin Pop. He started his singing career
as a member of the boy band Menudo. Later, he would leave
the group for a solo career. He released ten solo albums and
another thirteen with Menudo. He has received two Grammy
Awards with eight nominations. He received three nominations for "Livin' la Vida Loca." He also has three Latin Grammy Awards, including one for his hit "She Bangs."

*L*A **V**IDA **L**OCA

¾ ounce crème de banana
¾ ounce cherry brandy
¾ ounce melon liqueur
¾ ounce coconut liqueur

Fill a cocktail glass with ice and water to chill. Fill the tin side of a Boston shaker with ice. Add the crème de banana, cherry brandy, melon liqueur, and coconut liqueur into the glass side of the shaker. Pour the liquid into the tin and attach the two sides. Shake until the sound of the ice changes and the combination is cold. Discard the ice and water in the cocktail glass. Strain the cocktail into the cocktail glass. Serve.

With fifteen studio albums, the British group Incognito has enjoyed success since the early 1980s. Their 1992 album *Tribes, Vibes and Scribes* and 1995 album *100° and Rising* are their greatest commercial successes. The band members have changed over the years, with band leader Jean-Paul Maunick (aka Bluey) remaining for the full run of the group.

/NCOGNITO

1 ½ ounces vodka
1 ounce apricot brandy
4 ounces ginger beer

Add ice to a Collins glass to chill the glass. Add the vodka, brandy, and ginger beer to the glass. Gently stir and serve.

Another incognito cocktail . . . for all the rock stars I did not mention in this book!

INCOGNITO

2 ounces of Lillet
1 ounce Cognac
⅓ ounce apricot brandy
1 dash of Angostura bitters

Add ice and water to a cocktail glass to chill the glass. Add ice to a mixing glass, then add the Angostura bitters, Lillet, brandy, and apricot brandy. Stir forty times. Empty the ice and water out of the glass and then strain the cocktail into the glass. Serve.

BIBLIOGRAPHY

Allen, Marvin J. *Magic in a Shaker: A Year of Spirited Libations*. Gretna, LA: Pelican, 2014.

Amis, Kingsley. *Everyday Drinking*. New York: Bloomsbury, 2008.

Arthur, Stanley Clisby. *Famous New Orleans Drinks and How to Mix 'Em*. Gretna, LA: Pelican, 1937, 1944, 1965, 1972, 2013.

Awards Websites:

https://www.rockhall.com/inductees

https://www.grammy.com/

http://awardsdatabase.oscars.org/

https://www.goldenglobes.com/winners-nominees

Beare, Emma, editor. *501 Must-Drink Cocktails*. London: Bounty Books, 2007.

Bullock, Tom. *The Ideal Bartender*. St. Louis: Buxton & Skinner, 1917.

Burke, Harman Burney. *Burke's Complete Cocktail & Drinking Recipes: With Recipes for Food Bits for the Cocktail Hour*. New York: Books, 1936.

Crockett, Albert Stevens. *The Old Waldorf-Astoria Bar Book*. New York: A. S. Crockett, 1935.

Daly, Tim. *Daly's Bartenders' Encyclopedia*. Worchester, MA: Tim Daly, 1903.

Dick, Erma Biesel. *The Old House: Holiday & Party Cookbook*. New York: Cowles, 1969.

Duecy, Erica. *Storied Sips: Evocative Cocktails for Everyday Escapes, with 40 Recipes*. New York: Random House Reference, 2013.

Embury, David. *The Fine Art of Mixing Drinks: The Classic Guide to the Cocktail*. New York: Mud Puddle Books, 2008, 2009.

Federle, Tim. *Tequila Mockingbird: Cocktails with a Literary Twist*. Philadelphia: Running Press, 2013.

Haigh, Ted (aka Dr. Cocktail). *Vintage Spirits and Forgotten Cocktails: From the Alamagoozlum to the Zombie and Beyond*. Beverly, MA: Quarry Books, 2009.

Hearn, Lafcadio. *La Cuisine Creole: A Collection of Culinary Recipes, From Leading Chefs and Noted Creole Housewives, Who Have Made New Orleans Famous for its Cuisine*. New Orleans: Hansell & Brothers, 1885.

Hess, Robert. *The Essential Bartender's Pocket Guide: Truly Great Cocktail Recipes*. New York: Mud Puddle Books, 2009.

Jackson, Michael. *Michael Jackson's Bar & Cocktail Companion: The Connoisseur's Handbook*. Philadelphia: Running Press, 1994.

Johnson, Harry. *Harry Johnson's 1882 New and Improved Bartender's Manual and a Guide for Hotels and Restaurants*. Newark, NJ: Charles E. Graham, 1882, 1934, 2008.

Kappeler, George J. *Modern American Drinks: How to Mix and Serve All Kinds of Cups and Drinks*. New York: Merriam, 1895, 2008.

Knorr, Paul. *10,000 Drinks*. New York: Sterling, 2007.

Kosmas, Jason, and Dushan Zaric. *Speakeasy: Classic Cocktails Reimagined, From New York's Employees Only Bar*. Berkeley, CA: Ten Speed Press, 2010.

Lipinski, Bob, and Kathie Lipinski. *The Complete Beverage Dictionary, 2nd edition*. New York: Van Nostrand Reinhold, 1996.

Meehan, Jim. *The PDT Cocktail Book: The Complete Bartender's Guide from the Celebrated Speakeasy*. New York: Sterling Epicure, 2011.

Miller, Dalyn, and Larry Donavan. *The Daily Cocktail: 365 Intoxicating Drinks and the Outrageous Events that Inspired Them*. Gloucester, MA: Fair Winds, 2006.

New York Bartenders' Association. *Official Handbook and Guide*. New York: New York Bartenders' Association, 1895.

Reed, Ben. *Ben Reed's Bartender's Guide*. New York: Ryland, Peters & Small, 2006.

Reekie, Jennie. *The London Ritz Book of Drinks: From Fine Wines and Fruit Punches to Cocktails and Canapés*. London: Ebury Press, 1990.

Rosenbaum, Stephanie. *The Art of Vintage Cocktails*. New York: Egg & Dart Press, 2013.

Schmid, Albert W. A. *The Kentucky Bourbon Cookbook*. Lexington, KY: University Press of Kentucky, 2010.

———. *The Manhattan Cocktail: A Modern Guide to the Whiskey Classic*. Lexington, KY: University Press of Kentucky, 2015.

———. *The Old Fashioned: An Essential Guide to the Original Whiskey Cocktail*. Lexington, KY: University Press of Kentucky, 2013.

———. *How to Drink Like a Mobster: Prohibition-Style Cocktails.* Bloomington, IN: Red Lighting Books, 2018.

———. *How to Drink Like a Spy.* Bloomington, IN: Red Lighting Books, 2018.

Stanforth, Deirdre. *The New Orleans Restaurant Cookbook: The Colorful History and Fabulous Cuisine of the Great Restaurants of New Orleans.* Garden City, NY: Doubleday, 1967.

Thomas, Jerry. *Bar-Tenders Guide: Containing Receipts for Mixing.* New York: Dick & Fitzgerald, 1887, 2008.

Trader Vic. *Trader Vic's Bartender's Guide, Revised.* Garden City, NY: Doubleday, 1947, 1972.

Wellmann, Molly. *Handcrafted Cocktails: The Mixologist's Guide to Classic Drinks for Morning, Noon & Night.* Cincinnati, OH: Betterway Home, 2013.

Wondrich, David. *Imbibe!* New York: Perigee, 2007.

ALBERT W. A. SCHMID is a Gourmand Award winner and author of several books, including *The Old Fashioned: An Essential Guide to the Original Whiskey Cocktail*; *The Manhattan Cocktail: A Modern Guide to the Whiskey Classic*; *How to Drink Like a Mobster*; and *The Hot Brown: Louisville's Legendary Open-Faced Sandwich*.